SPEAK
WITH
POWER
AND
GRACE

SPEAK
WITH
POWER
AND
GRACE

*A Woman's Guide to
Public Speaking*

Linda D. Swink

Foreword by Richard L. Weaver II

Skyhorse Publishing

Skyhorse Publishing books may be purchased in bulk at special discounts for sales promotion, corporate gifts, fund-raising, or educational purposes. Special editions can also be created to specifications. For details, contact the Special Sales Department, Skyhorse Publishing, 307 West 36th Street, 11th Floor, New York, NY 10018 or info@skyhorsepublishing.com.

Skyhorse® and Skyhorse Publishing® are registered trademarks of Skyhorse Publishing, Inc.®, a Delaware corporation.

Visit our website at www.skyhorsepublishing.com.

10 9 8 7 6 5 4 3 2 1

Library of Congress Cataloging-in-Publication Data is available on file.
ISBN: 978-1-62636-424-0

Printed in the United States of America.

To my husband and my mother
for their continuous love and support,
and to Toastmasters everywhere
for all their help, encouragement, and friendship

I thank the wonderful women of the
Central Ohio Fiction Writers in Columbus, Ohio,
for helping me understand what this
writing business is all about.

Foreword

The ability to speak effectively—to be listened to by those who matter—is crucial for success. And with women now occupying close to fifty percent of workplace positions, it is critically important for women to be able to communicate with skill and assurance.

Women deserve a book especially for them, written by someone who knows, who cares, and who has been there. Linda is just such a person. That is why a handy, practical guide like this one is so valuable. To have one written by a female professional speaker is like icing on the cake!

Several factors motivated me to write this foreword. First, I am intimately interested in Linda's topic. Second, in my work of training hundreds of graduate teaching assistants in speech communication and teaching thousands of students, I am always looking for new, exciting ideas to share with others. Third, as a practicing writer and speaker who has had nine speeches included in *Vital Speeches of the Day,* and who has had more than ninety articles published, I feel I am in a unique position to evaluate Linda's work.

Whether you're a beginner or a veteran, Linda's book satisfies. It quiets the fears of the unknown. It forces you to resist the temptation of procrastination. It quickens the sluggish brain. Also, it keeps you believing you have something worthwhile to say. Through study and practice, time and effort, commitment and dedication—like anyone who wants to excel—effective speakers must invest in the fundamentals. Don't believe the myth that good speakers are born, not made. It's a lie. Public speaking is an ability that can be learned. Good speakers become good speakers through desire, effort, and practice.

As a student of public speaking who has a library of thousands of related books, I consider this one outstanding because of its relevance, because of its breadth, because of its practical, sensible advice, and because it is written by a woman for women. From the beginning, Linda shares, step by step, how to put a speech together. The emphasis is on women from the opening chapter when she explains ways women can overcome fear of public speaking, questions to ask before beginning a speech, and specific suggestions for writing the speech. Linda traces each part of the process and answers the most often asked questions: How do you make the right moves? What is unique about the female voice, and how do women speakers capitalize on their uniqueness? What platform techniques work best? What is proper etiquette in front of an audience? What are special concerns for women at the lectern? How do you handle distractions? And how can you best adapt to special circumstances? Linda, too, offers useful examples, tips, and personal experiences that, by themselves, make this volume worth its price.

Seldom have I read a book with as much down-to-earth, effective guidance on effective public speaking. Linda presents specific, detailed information. Take time to digest the book's content; then put the suggestions to use in your next speech. By applying the principles and using the techniques in this book, you will be more successful at any job that requires clear communication. You will learn to enjoy public speaking more and fear it less.

This is a volume you will read again and again. It will help you become the best public speaker you can be. Yes, it is truly *that* good!

Dr. Richard L. Weaver II, Professor
Department of Interpersonal Communication
Bowling Green State University, Ohio

Preface

During my twenty-some odds years as a professional speaker, I have had the pleasure of training hundreds of women to become more confident at the lectern. Many attended my workshops and seminars uncertain of how to make a speech: some were fearful that they weren't up to the task and others were just plain terrorized at the prospect of standing before a group of strangers and talking to them.

Some of the comments I heard were: "I could never give a speech. I'd be scared to death with all those eyes staring at me."

"Me, give a speech? Are you crazy? I'd rather die. In fact, I'm sure I would."

"I'll forget everything I wanted to say and make a fool of myself."

These concerns about public speaking are far too common, and unfortunately are the seeds of failure. But the opposite is true. The public speaking experience is an opportunity that can lead to promotions, career enhancements, and personal growth; in others words—success.

The ability to influence, inspire, and motivate others and to effectively express your ideas and opinions means the difference between climbing that corporate ladder of success or remaining in a go-nowhere job. Yet for many women, the thought of making a speech before a group of strangers sends a paralyzing fear through their bodies that shakes their self-confidence and causes them to avoid stepping on that first rung of that ladder. Because of that fear, they beg off making a speech, leaving their jobs hanging in jeopardy.

There are women who will scribble a few notes on a scrap of paper, run the information quickly through their heads, present the speech, and then wonder why they failed. That's why we hear so many tedious, boring, ill-prepared speeches—the speaker didn't know how to prepare a speech, hadn't honed her delivery skills, and simply wasn't ready.

Still other women believe that just because they can talk, they can make a speech.

Ben Jonson, English dramatist and poet, said, "Talking and eloquence are not the same; to speak, and to speak well are two different things." Talking is like a slow dripping water faucet. Making a speech is akin to a rushing waterfall—more energetic, more interesting, and certainly more powerful.

No one expects to read a book about playing golf, then rush to join a professional golf league. Nor would they show up at Carnegie Hall expecting to play the piano without first investing many years into practicing the scales. Yet some women feel they can deliver a formal presentation without putting time in preparation and practice because they feel they can "wing it." Without the speaker knowing the techniques for a powerful delivery and without preparation, planning, and practice, the presentation is doomed to fail.

Public speaking is a learned skill much like driving a car. Remember the first time you got behind the wheel? You sat staring at the instrument panel, heart racing, palms sweating. A thousand worries flashed through your head. What if I run over something or someone? What if I hit another car? What if...? Yes, driving for the first time was a scary, frightening experience. But with the desire of obtaining your driver's license you started the engine. With practice you gained confidence, you drove the car to the grocery store—then to the mall across town. Before long, you had the courage to drive at night, and later in the rain and snow.

Making a speech follows the same principle. It takes hours of work to turn a few scribbled notes into a successful speech. You cannot expect to stand before an audience the first time and present a one-hour speech as skillfully as a professional. But with the proper preparation and practice, you can begin making shorter speeches that give you the self-confidence to tackle longer and more intricate presentations.

Take the necessary risks that accompany any unknown venture and take advantage of every opportunity. Be ready for those opportunities when they come, and never quit because you think you might fail. Author Anne Morrow Lindbergh said, "It takes as much courage to have tried and failed as it does to have tried and succeeded."

Speak With Power and Grace: A Woman's Guide to Public Speaking provides information for two types of presenters: the novice and the experienced speaker. For the novice, it answers the puzzling questions of where to begin, how to create and present a speech that looks and sounds like a well polished presentation. For the experienced speaker who may want to improve her presentation style, it shows how to add more pizzazz and punch to an already developed speech by using the techniques of the professional speaker.

This book examines the basic elements of public speaking from the beginning stages of preparing a speech to organizing and writing the text. It explores platform techniques and etiquette and the special concerns women face at the lectern. Special attention is given to using voice and body language. The section on humor, making the executive briefing, and how to appear before the camera are an added bonus.

Throughout the book, I incorporate advice and experiences from experts in the field of communication. Professional female speakers tell how they handle problems during a presentation and I reveal many of my experiences—good and bad—in front of audiences.

Since the first edition of this book, technology has changed, making parts of the section on visual aids and microphones obsolete. The wireless lavaliere has, for all practical purposes, replaced the handheld microphone, and it's not uncommon to see speakers using a wireless head microphone. Still the suggestion I give for handling and using the microphone still applies.

PowerPoint, for the most part, has replaced the use of 35mm slides and overhead projectors. Learning to use PowerPoint takes computer savvy, but can make the difference between an ordinary speech and a dynamic presentation. As with visual aids, the rules in making and handling should not be ignored.

Who needs this book? *Speak With Power and Grace: A Woman's Guide to Public Speaking* is for every woman who has ever had to get up in front of a group of people to speak and found she lacked confidence and skill. This includes the secretary of the garden club who reads the minutes of last month's meeting, sales people, managers and supervisors, professional educators, health care professionals, religious and political leaders, and the woman who wants her voice heard at city hall. In short, every woman needing and wanting to learn better public speaking skills will find this book a valuable guide. No matter what your goal—whether it's to gain control of your nervousness, to learn how to prepare, organize, and deliver a speech, or to polish and refine your present skills— this book is for you.

Who am I to tell you how to give a speech? I have trained executives, managers, secretaries, dietitians, records clerks, bank executives, doctors, educators, and women just like you who wanted more than to just give a talk. They wanted to be successful at it because it meant the difference between a mediocre job and a successful career. I have taken "Nervous Nellies" and transformed them into confident, poised, and polished speakers.

Several of my articles on public speaking have appeared in *The Toastmaster,* a magazine for the international organization of public speakers and communication leaders. And, aside from wanting to see women succeed, I have a personal interest in seeing that you learn these skills and become a better speaker: I may have to sit and listen to you speak one day.

One final note: There isn't a magic formula in this book, but there is straightforward advice. You can learn from it, but you will have to do the work. Nothing great ever comes without effort. Learning any new skill takes time. You must practice what I present in these chapters, not just once or twice, but repeatedly. You say you don't have years to practice because you have to make a presentation next week? Well, what are you waiting for? Let's get started.

PART I

Preparation

Overcoming the Fear
of Public Speaking

*You gain strength, courage, and confidence by every
experience in which you really stop to look fear in the face.*

ELEANOR ROOSEVELT, *You Learn by Living*

I ask women in my workshops why they dislike speaking in
public. They say:

"I'm afraid I'll make a mistake and look foolish."

"I'll bore the audience."

"I don't like that awful nervous feeling I get in my stomach."

"I fear that my mind will go blank, and I'll just stand there
looking stupid."

"I don't want to look bad in front of my boss. He's very
critical."

"I don't feel comfortable with all those eyes watching me."

"My voice gets shaky and people can see I'm nervous."

"It just scares me. I'm afraid something will go wrong."

Their answers seldom reveal any surprises. These are real concerns to the women making each statement, and that last reason—fearing the unknown—is the most common.

Although these fears seem real, they are misguided. Zig Ziglar, professional speaker, says fear is False Evidence Appearing Real—meaning that the fear you have about what you *think* might happen or what you *think* might go wrong while you are speaking is irrational.

Dr. David D. Burns, in *The Feeling Good Handbook*, says there is a difference between healthy fear and neurotic anxiety. "The thoughts that lead to healthy fear are realistic; they alert us to dangers that we need to deal with." In other words, healthy fear would prevent us from going skydiving without a parachute. Anticipating disastrous results, we would make sure we had a parachute and that it was packed correctly. Likewise, we know that unless we take the necessary actions to prepare for a speech, we could go splat like an ill-equipped skydiver.

Burns also says that neurotic anxiety is the result of distorted thoughts that have little basis in reality. Some people fear getting up in front of an audience to speak because they believe they will have an attack of the "frights" and might die. A neurotic anxiety is akin to worrying about a meteor falling from the sky and landing on your head. Although the possibility is extremely unlikely, you build a fortified underground bunker with a meteor detector on top, just for assurance. Worrying about things that probably will never happen, or even worrying excessively about setbacks that may occur, is a waste of energy. That energy could be put to better use preparing and practicing your speech.

Both healthy fear and neurotic anxiety may be triggered by having to speak in public. The healthy fears and concerns you have are good. You know things can go wrong, but with proper planning you can deal with and fix anything that might happen. When you understand that nothing is so bad that you cannot deal with it, the fear is diminished and you begin controlling your nervousness. Once you learn to control those butterflies, you're on your way to success. Unfortunately, the only cure for neurotic anxiety is to seek professional help.

You may understand the difference between healthy fear and neurotic anxiety, but still get nervous. What can you do? Before you can begin controlling your nervousness, you must understand what causes those jitters.

NINE KEY INGREDIENTS
TO CONTROLLING NERVOUSNESS

Nervousness is a basic human reaction to a stressful situation, fear, or anxiety. When you feel threatened, adrenaline pumps into your system, preparing you to control the danger or run for your life. Those adrenaline-pumping pistons really do a job.

Being apprehensive about making a speech is normal—in fact, it has several benefits—so you shouldn't try to eliminate those scary feelings completely. You want a twinge of nervousness because, first, it heightens your awareness of the situation, causing you to want to do well, and, second, that extra adrenaline makes you appear energetic and enthusiastic.

You need to worry when you become complacent. A speaker who doesn't care about how well she'll do will have no energy, no enthusiasm, and will surely anesthetize an audience. Nervousness manifests itself at various times and in different ways. For me, it's the day before the speech. My stomach knots as I begin to worry if I'm ready. I keep asking, have I done everything possible to make my speech the best? Do I have all my handouts, visual aids, and notes?

You will always experience some level of nervousness either before or while making a speech. The trick is to learn to control it. Although you may feel as though you're going to pass out from fright, trust me, it won't happen.

I wish I had a magic wand I could wave over your head while saying, "Go forth and never be nervous about speaking in public again." Sorry, it just doesn't work that way. Once you know the basics and begin practicing them, you'll gain confidence. With more confidence, you'll start controlling those nervous jitters and become more comfortable speaking before an audience. Once you become comfortable, look out! You may discover you enjoy public speaking.

There is no simple one-step miracle method for overcoming fear, but there are things that will help you better understand why you become nervous and what you can do about it.

1. *The first key ingredient to taking control of those feelings is to understand that everyone gets butterflies before making a speech.* We all experience stage fright to some degree; some more than others. You aren't the only one who gets a quivering stomach and shaky knees; even professional actors and athletes get stage fright. You wouldn't think a 225-pound football player would have anything to be nervous about, but Mike Pruitt, former running back for the Cleveland Browns, said he became anxious before every game, and his anxiety intensified the day of the game. Actress Marla Gibbs says hiding behind her character gives her confidence. Musician Billy Joel gets opening-night jitters, worrying about forgetting the words to the song, and singer and actress Bette Midler says she stays so busy before a performance she doesn't have time to think about being nervous.

Sure these performers get nervous, but their audiences can't tell. Each has developed personal techniques to excel without being hampered by nervousness. They have learned to turn their concerns into a positive force. You can, too. The next time you think you're out there by yourself, feeling like a bundle of nerves, tell yourself, "I'm not alone. Everyone in my audience who has ever given a speech has felt this way. Feeling nervous is normal; it's good because it tells me I'm ready to make the best speech ever."

2. *The next ingredient is to understand that it's okay to make a mistake.* Nathalia Crane, author of *Imperfection*, said, "There is a glory in a great mistake."

We're all human. We make mistakes. We learn and grow from our failures. Accept that fact and *plan to make mistakes.* Plan to make mistakes?! Yes, preparing for and knowing what to do should you make a mistake gives you confidence. With each speaking experience comes knowledge of how to prevent the same thing happening again.

It's not the end of the world if you blunder; it's how you handle the situation that counts. You say you forgot an entire section of your speech, you became tongue-tied and stumbled over a word, or you dropped your notes? Don't worry. The sun will rise tomorrow. Later in this book I'll show you how to handle each of those problems. For now, knowing it's all right to make mistakes and that you can recover from them should raise your confidence level.

Besides, fretting about it is worse than the actual mistake itself. If you worry long enough, you'll begin believing you'll make a mistake and actually cause it to happen—the self-fulfilling prophecy in action.

3. *Understand that it's all right to be the center of attention.* Although everyone likes to be noticed, few people like being stared at. As children we were told it wasn't polite to act up in front of people. How many times did your mother or father tell you not to show off because people were watching? We were made to feel that being the center of attention was somehow wrong. We grew up believing it. Now, as adults, when we have to speak in front of people, we hear those phantom words, "Stop showing off! People are watching."

Many women, though, have learned to turn being the center of attention into a high art form. They are the women who succeed because they have charm, charisma, and a sense of self-worth. They love the "limelight" and aren't afraid to show the world just who they are—leaders. They use the attention to move forward, focusing on a goal rather than self.

4. *Don't take yourself or the speaking situation too seriously.* I recall giving a speech where I stood at the head table with the officers of the club seated to my left and right. Just as I began speaking there was a loud crash, dead silence, then snickering from the audience. The woman sitting next to me had fallen from her broken chair. I was so involved in my opening remarks, I didn't notice her sprawled on the floor. It was only after she tugged on the hem of my skirt that I knew what had happened. She wasn't hurt—more embarrassed than anything

else. After the audience had settled down and the broken chair had been replaced, I remarked, "A speech teacher of mine once said, 'The opening of your speech should knock them off their seats.' I don't think this is exactly what he had in mind."

A speaker with less experience or little confidence might have been deeply upset by this experience. You can't allow that to happen.

5. *Adopt a positive attitude.* Many books have been written about the power of positive thinking. This isn't a new concept. Nothing can be more self-defeating for you, as a woman, than a negative attitude about yourself or your abilities. Sure you may not be the best—right now—but keep telling yourself you're going to be great, and someday you will be.

When you tell yourself you *can* do something, like the little train that said, "I think I can, I think I can," you'll soon discover you can do whatever you set your mind to. Dorothy Sarnoff, speech coach and author, calls this "channeling your belief system." She says repeat to yourself, "I'm glad I'm here. I'm glad you're here. I know what I know and I care about you." She says that by repeating these thoughts, you can alter your belief system and begin to believe what you program into your brain.

So, the next time you're faced with having to make a speech, begin by saying, "I want to do this because it's important. This is a great opportunity to help others. I can do it. I want to do it. I'm going to do it, and I'm going to be great."

6. *Know your subject inside and out, backward and forward.* You can't possibly feel comfortable or confident when speaking on a subject foreign to you. The more you know and understand about your topic, the more confidence you'll have in your ability to deliver that information and to answer any tricky questions that might be hurled at you. You won't have to worry about losing your place or forgetting what you intended to say; with a glance at your notes to jog your memory, you'll be able to continue with confidence.

7. *Prepare well for every speaking situation by answering the twenty-six questions in chapter 2.*

8. *Gain experience.* You're too nervous to give a speech, so you can't get experience? Yes, you can. Speaking to small groups will help reduce nervousness and prepare you for more complex speaking situations. Every time you give a report at work, read the minutes of a meeting, or simply make an announcement, think of it as making a speech. You're saying prepared words to a group of people. That's a speech. That's experience. You'll find that the more experiences you get, the less threatening and stressful speaking becomes, and the more courage you'll gain. Eleanor Roosevelt said, "I believe anyone can conquer fear by doing the things he fears to do, provided he keeps doing them until he has a record of successful experiences behind him."

9. *Finally, the most important key: Practice, practice, practice.* Practice using gestures that help illustrate your story. Practice using visual aids until you are comfortable with them. Practice vocal variety for a more powerful delivery. Begin practicing, not the night before, but days, even weeks, before the scheduled date of your presentation. With each rehearsal you work out the kinks and problems and gain confidence.

THE KEY INGREDIENTS OF A GOOD SPEECH

The key ingredient of any speech is the speaker. A successful speaker is completely familiar with her topic. To augment her prior knowledge of the subject, she gathers additional information to support her presentation. Author and lecturer Dale Carnegie suggested that speakers should know ten times more information about their subject than they plan to use.

A successful speaker has done her homework. She knows her audience and what her speaking environment will be like. She's organized, with notes and visual aids ready before she steps up to the lectern. She presents information in a logical, lively, and easy-to-understand manner, using a pleasant voice, the kind of voice that could lull a baby to sleep but keeps an audience awake, eager for more.

She's truly enthusiastic. An audience can detect phony enthusiasm. She's confident in her ability and poised as she stands before her audience. Her smile reveals that she's friendly and sincere in her efforts to present information. She speaks with conviction and honesty. She has energy as she moves and gestures, making her speech spark with electricity.

A successful speaker is well-prepared. She checks and rechecks all her information, presents everything pertinent to the subject, and never begins a presentation without having spent considerable time practicing the speech.

Most of all, a good speaker is flexible. Why? Because Murphy sits lurking in the wings, waiting for just the right moment to spring out and cause havoc. Remember Murphy's Law, which states, "If anything can go wrong, it will and at the most inappropriate time and usually in triplicate." You must be ready for anything to go wrong, anytime, anywhere. The more flexible you are, the better you'll be at handling any problem that comes along.

Finally, a good speaker stays in tip-top condition physically, mentally, spiritually, and morally. She has physical energy to move with vitality, mental agility to handle those crazy things that happen to all speakers, and spiritual reserves in times of stress and disaster. Her moral character—who she is when no one is looking—accompanies her to the lectern.

2

The Who, What, Where, When, and How of Preparing a Speech

The breathtaking part of it all was not so much the planning as the fantastic skill with which the planning was concealed.

EVA LE GALLIENNE, *The Mystic in the Theatre*

I have heard many stories of tricks used by speakers to get them through their speech, such as wearing lucky socks or carrying a special good-luck charm, buying a new outfit, pretending the audience wasn't there, even picturing the audience in their underwear—or naked. These tricks give a false sense of confidence and seem to work for those believing in them, but they cannot sustain a speaker for long, nor can they replace the hours of preparation needed to produce a good speech. I cannot stress strongly enough the importance of preparation. Speaking without preparing is like shooting without taking aim. You may connect with some of your audience, but chances are you'll shoot yourself in the foot.

It's important to know what contributes to a first-rate speech. A top-quality speech is easy to understand, clear, and logical. It is well organized, with an opening, a body, and a conclusion. It has a definite purpose, follows a single theme with one point of view, and is thoroughly prepared and rehearsed. An excellent speech is not a mechanical process of presenting information. It is not an oratorical performance, and it is not a reading.

Properly planning a speech lets you see where you're going so you can lay out the best route to get there. Planning also identifies potential problems early, giving you a chance to solve them before they lead to disaster. Eliminating problems before they occur saves you needless hours of worry.

Mediocre preparation produces a mediocre presentation. Although preparation is the most important factor in giving a speech, it is often the least considered. For that reason, I have compiled a comprehensive list of questions to guide you in planning your speech.

There are two types of questions: those you should ask yourself and those you may ask of the person who has invited you to speak.

TWENTY-SIX QUESTIONS YOU NEED TO ASK BEFORE YOU BEGIN

1. *Who is my contact person?* Your contact person provides the foundation for the success of your presentation. He or she knows what the audience expects, has all the information regarding the facilities where you're to speak, and can give you details of the program and the arrangements being made. So, first ask, "What is his or her name, and at what phone numbers can he or she be reached?"

The following questions are in no specific order. Some are more important than others, some may not apply to your speaking situation, but all should be given consideration.

2. *What is the purpose or objective of my speech or presentation?* Many women fail to deliver a successful presentation

because they don't have a clearly defined purpose in mind when they start out. You must know and fully understand what you want to achieve by making the speech and what you want the audience to think, feel, or do as a result of hearing it. Do you want to persuade your audience to place an order, write a letter, vote, or believe in a new concept or idea? Do you wish to inform, motivate, or solve a problem? Is your audience expecting you to entertain them, or to inspire them? Knowing what you want to achieve and focusing on a specific purpose will make your speech more successful.

3. *Who is my audience?* An audience is like a patchwork quilt with each piece a different color, size, pattern, shape, and background, all held together by a common thread. Knowing the makeup of your audience allows you to tailor information to their specific needs, level of understanding, interests, and expectations.

Approach your speech from the audience's perspective and stay audience-focused. You need to ask, "What does my audience want?" "Does my speech satisfy that need?"

Look at the overall message. Have you given your audience something meaningful to take home, something they'll remember and use, something that will make their lives better? Too often, speakers build speeches around an idea or topic that is of importance only to themselves. What's wrong with that, you ask? Isn't that what you're supposed to do—speak about something that is of interest and importance to you? Absolutely, but your message must be centered around the audience's need for that information, not around the message itself. Your message must relate directly to, and focus on, the concerns of your audience because they'll be asking, "What's in it for me?"

Analyze the demographics of the audience. What is the age and sex ratio of your audience? What is their educational level, profession or occupation, and socioeconomic background? Depending on your topic, you may need to know their religion, race, and marital status. You'll need to be aware of their cultural heritage and what political and social affiliations they have. What do they already know about your topic? The more they know, the less you need to explain. Will they be hostile toward the topic? What are their special interests, concerns, problems, likes and dislikes? Each audience will require a different approach, different visual aids, and a different speaking style, with a different language, stories, and analogies.

For example, each age group has different perspectives, personal experiences, needs, attitudes, and goals. What works well for a group of senior citizens will not always work for a younger group. A younger audience is more trusting and more willing to accept new ideas. An older audience is more likely to question your motives and is less easily swayed. A typed handout may be fine for a twenty- to forty-year-old audience, but may not be readable by older people, many of whom may have impaired vision. A walk down memory lane will appeal to the older crowd, but don't ask today's teenagers to recall the day John F. Kennedy died. Also keep in mind that interests and points of view change with age.

Men and women communicate and think differently. (Now, there's an understatement.) According to Judith C. Tingley, Ph.D., president of Judith C. Tingley, Ph.D. Associates, a consulting firm, women tend to express themselves in terms of feelings, relationships, and nurturing. Men, on the other hand, think in terms of business success and power plays.

Although the male/female roles have blurred, males tend to tune in to topics that relate to business, money, or sports. A woman delivering a speech to a male audience should use anecdotes and metaphors that relate to these topics.

Suzette Elgin, author of *The Last Word on the Gentle Art of Verbal Self-Defense*, says, "When men and women don't make some adaptation in their speech pattern to the other gender, whether to an individual or a large audience, they are guaranteed to fail."

Also, look at your audience as a group. What do they have in common? Does the audience belong to a professional association? Are they from the same company or type of business? Are they management people or members of organized labor? Is the group a social club or a military organization? Get to know about their organization. Talk to the members, the secretary, or the president of the group. What are their special interests, needs, and concerns? Are they facing a special problem in their company or club? Find out if their meetings are structured or informal and learn the customs of the group. Read their newsletters and brochures. Learn their mission statement, slogan, song, or creed.

Although the members may belong to the same organization, each chapter may be different. A Rotary club in a rural community may be more conservative or informal than one in a city where members are more business oriented. Each will require a different approach, even though they have the same mission as a group.

Ask if anyone of prominence, such as a political leader or the boss, will be in attendance. If he or she likes you, it's a good bet the rest of the group will too. You also need to know who will be in your audience so you can make a proper greeting in your opening remarks.

What is your relationship to the audience? Are they coworkers, subordinates, colleagues, customers, or your superiors? Is this audience voluntary or captive?

An audience's proximity to your subject is also something to consider. How much do they care about your topic? In what way does the subject touch their lives?

One last thing about audiences. You aren't going to reach every person all of the time. The best you can hope for is to please the majority most of the time.

4. *What type of speech am I expected to make?* Basically, there are four types of speeches: informative, entertaining, inspirational, and motivational. The type of speech you make is directly related to the purpose of your speech. For example, an introduction is informative. An after-dinner speech is entertaining as well as informative, and a keynote address should enlighten and inspire the audience. A sales talk is motivational because its purpose is to persuade the audience to buy a service or product.

5. *What is the occasion?* Just as each type of speech has different requirements, each occasion is different in tone and mood, setting, seating arrangement, visual aids and equipment, and planning approach.

Is the occasion the weekly meeting of a service club such as the Kiwanis or Lions? Is it an executive briefing, a training seminar or workshop, or an all-day conference? Is the event a fiftieth wedding anniversary, a dedication of a building, a luncheon for the ladies auxiliary, or a retirement ceremony? Is the occasion a trade show, a political rally or fund-raiser, or a roast?

Will you be speaking at a city council meeting, board meeting, graduation, or funeral? Will you be accepting or presenting an award, welcoming a new member to your staff or saying goodbye to a colleague or speaking at a news conference?

6. *How do I choose a topic?* No matter what topic you choose, there is one rule that is absolute: Speak on a subject that excites you, that you truly believe in, and that is important to your audience, but most of all, *speak on what you know.* Speak about things you know from firsthand experience. There is a belief among fiction writers that you can't tell someone else's story. You can never tell it the same way as someone who lived it or gave birth to the plot. The same is true for speakers. Do your own research, gather your own information, and do your own interviews. Tell your own personal stories.

A friend of mine was speaking to the members of a local service club about how to conduct an interview. She seemed ill at ease. During her speech she commented that she was nervous but didn't understand why, because she had spoken to this group before and hadn't been nervous then. She let it slip that she was talking on a subject that was of importance to her husband (he worked in human resources). She was reading from his notes, and remembering what he had said while talking to her about the subject. Her job experience was in day care. She was out of her element and it showed. Later, I asked her why she thought she was nervous. She replied, "I felt as if I were just mouthing words." Her message didn't come from her heart or her own experience.

In many work-related speaking situations your topic will be chosen for you. You may be asked to brief staff members about procedural changes and company policies, explain to colleagues how to perform your job, or give a progress update or sales report. You may be required to speak to the media about your company's latest achievements.

If you're asked to speak to a group, generally it's because you have special knowledge that others want or need. Maybe you have an unusual hobby, such as collecting pictures of creative mailboxes. Maybe you're the only female champion glider pilot in the state.

As a member of a service club or organization, you may be asked to speak on behalf of the group. Your topic could include the club's history, its purpose, membership requirements, and the benefits of belonging.

The more interested in and knowledgeable about the topic you are, the more enthusiasm you'll have for presenting that information.

7. *What objections does the audience have concerning my topic?* You may be placed in a situation where you have to speak to a hostile audience on a controversial subject. Be ready with plenty of support material to back you up. Have all your facts and figures ready and be prepared for a rough time if your audience has opposing viewpoints.

8. *What additional research and information will I need for this audience?* Every speech and audience requires different information. Round out and update your talk with facts, statistics, quotes, illustrations, anecdotes, and appropriate humor to make it more interesting and palatable to this specific audience.

First, draw on personal knowledge of the subject. You have a wealth of information stored in that mental computer. Review what you already know, then ask yourself where you can find additional information. Talk to the experts. Maybe you heard or read somewhere about someone who has done research on your topic. Write or call that person. Set up an interview with him or her. Most people are willing, even delighted, to share information. Don't be surprised if you get more information than you plan to use. Save those gems for another speech.

Always ask permission to use an interviewee's quotes, and be sure to give him or her credit in your speech. Using expert testimony adds credibility to your presentation.

Make the local library a frequent stop. Start by looking through books, encyclopedias, magazines, almanacs, professional journals, newspapers, and copies of others' speeches. Don't overlook government studies, business reports, and company brochures. Gather recent statistics to make your claims stronger; cross-check them for accuracy. Always look for something new, a different slant, and never pass up the humorous anecdote. If you live near a university, you'll have the additional resource of doctoral dissertations to consult.

Researching additional material can be tedious, but if you enjoy your subject, finding new information can be exciting. The many hours of extra research will pay off with a more believable presentation. Start collecting those jokes, stories, and interesting pieces of trivia today.

9. *How many people will I be speaking to?* Knowing the size of the audience helps you to visualize as you rehearse and to know which visual aids to use and how many handouts to make. A large audience calls for more volume, so a microphone will be necessary. If you're speaking to a large group, you'll need to practice using larger gestures than if you were speaking to a smaller group.

Small audiences of five to ten people lend themselves to an informal atmosphere, while larger numbers tend to be more formal. There are exceptions, of course. Executive briefings usually are small in number but formal in presentation style.

It seems natural to feel more nervous at the thought of speaking to a large crowd, but the opposite could be true. Personally, I feel more confident when speaking to a large group and uncomfortable when speaking to only one or two people. I look at it this way: If I am speaking to two people and can't convince one person, I have lost 50 percent of my audience. But if I'm speaking to five hundred and lose only one person, I'm still a success.

10. *What kind of room will I be speaking in?* Before you begin to gather information, organize material, or practice your speech, you must find out about the speaking environment. You need to know if you'll be speaking in a restaurant where there might be the distraction of rattling dishes and servers going in and out. Will you be speaking in a classroom, an echoing cafeteria, a hotel ballroom, a meeting hall, an auditorium, a church basement, or outdoors? Each type of environment has different requirements and problems that you'll need to consider before finalizing the preparations. This is important for several reasons.

Knowing what the room looks like ahead of time enables you to visualize it during practice and helps control nervousness when the time comes to actually deliver your speech. By then you have been in that room, albeit mentally, many times.

Second, you can prepare with certain expectations confirmed. You'll know how much room you have to move around on the podium, and if your visual aids are coordinated with the meeting room. You can anticipate problems, such as a post in the middle of the room that hinders the audience's view or chairs that can't be rearranged for your brainstorming session. Don't leave yourself open for a big surprise when you show up and discover you can't show the slides you so arduously prepared because the room can't be darkened.

So visit the location and see firsthand what the room looks like. If that's not possible, ask the chairperson the following:

• How far will you have to carry your visual aids and equipment from the parking lot? Is the room conveniently located near restrooms and water fountains?

• What size is the room? Will you be speaking in a convention hall with a vast stage and audience area, or in a small conference room? You'll want to know if the visual aids you plan

to use will work, if you'll need a microphone, and if the room
fits the size of the audience and the mood of your speech.

Is the room longer than it is wide, or is it square? Long, narrow rooms with people seated at one long table present sightline problems for both you and the audience. With a wide room,
you have another problem. As you talk to one section of the
room, the other side will be seeing your back or profile. Your
eye contact must expand from a normal 45 degrees to a possible 140 degrees. That's a tough room to talk to for an inexperienced speaker.

• Where is the door? Doors in the back of the room cause
few problems, but doors in front, especially near the lectern,
cause distractions every time someone comes in late. You don't
need that distraction. Ask that the seats be turned to face the
other direction, if possible.

• Will I be speaking on a podium? How many steps are
there? Will you be able to ascend the steps gracefully in a skirt?

• Will there be a curtain behind me? If so, what color? Most
curtains are dark, but the color may be blue, burgundy, green,
black, or other. Consider the color so you can coordinate the
color of your clothing with the background. A red suit against a
burgundy curtain is deadly, as are some greens against royal
blue. Black against black doesn't show up well. Also, watch out
for patterned brick walls and floral wallpapers.

• Is the room wheelchair accessible? If you need special facilities to enhance your mobility, you're already familiar with asking these questions. If you will speak while seated in a
wheelchair, let the meeting planner know you prefer to speak
on a riser, to give your audience better visibility. Ask that the
lectern be moved to one side so you can speak from the center of the platform.

Other things you need to check are:

• Acoustics: Will the room absorb your voice? Will it echo?
Whether your voice will carry on its own without a microphone
must be considered above all else.

• Windows: Do the windows have shades or drapes? You won't be able to show slides if the windows can't be covered. Sun shining through can cause glare, and bare windows don't absorb sound.

• Lighting: How well can the audience see to take notes? How well can you see the audience and your notes? Some rooms have no control over the houselights; they're either on or off, while others have control switches for different sections of the room and stage area. Some have dimmer switches controlling the amount of light in the room. Can the lights be dimmed by you or will you have to ask someone in the back of the room for assistance?

Many speakers want to see the faces of their audience and prefer not to speak in a darkened room. If you can't see the audience, you can't read their feedback or see a hand raised to ask a question; plus a darkened room can induce drowsiness especially after a meal.

• Electrical outlets: Are outlets located near the speaking area or will extension cords be necessary?

• The sound system and microphone: Is the facility equipped with a good-quality sound system and microphone? Will you have to bring your own?

• Can you control the room temperature? Will a noisy air conditioner spoil your presentation? I spoke once where there was such a monster. The coordinator turned the roaring air conditioner off but then the room got too hot. I had to choose between two handicaps. I chose to speak more loudly, over the roar of the air conditioner, rather than have my audience sit fanning themselves.

11. *Will there be a lectern, and if so, what kind, and where will it be positioned?* There are two types of lecterns: table and floor model. (I need to make a distinction before I continue. There is a difference between a lectern and a podium. A *lectern*, according to Webster's, is a stand having an inclined, shelflike surface on which a speaker may place books, papers, or notes.

A *podium*, on the other hand, is a small platform, riser, or dais for the conductor of an orchestra or a speaker to stand on. It is a solid foundation that supports a structure. Sometimes the word "podium" is used mistakenly when a lectern is meant. I am pointing this out now so you will know which I'm referring to in each case.)

• Where will the lectern be positioned? If you're the guest speaker at a formal banquet or after lunch or dinner, most likely you'll be seated at the head table and will speak from behind a table-model lectern. However, you might be expected to speak from another place in the room, behind a floor model.

• Does the lectern have a light attached? Does it work? You don't want to refer to your notes and not be able to see them. If the light doesn't work and can't be fixed, carry a penlight in your emergency bag so you can see your notes.

12. *How will the audience be seated?* Theater-style with raked seating, semi-circle, banquet-style, or conference-style? What kind of chairs are in the room—soft, contour chairs with padded arms or hard, folding chairs? Are the chairs movable? Will there be tables? What kind and in what arrangement? Are they small individual tables, long tables, or school desks?

The seating arrangement should match your presentation. If you plan to have your audience divide into smaller groups for a "think session," you'll need movable chairs. With a formal speech, theater-type seating works fine, but if you want your audience to take notes, they'll need something to write on besides their laps. While you're at it, make sure there are enough chairs for everyone. You don't want folks standing for your one-hour speech.

Unlike the professional speaker who charges big bucks for an hour of his or her time, you probably won't be able to do much about the room or make changes in the seating arrangements for your fifteen-minute speech to a local service club. You will have to make do with the way the room is set up. That's even more reason to check out the room beforehand.

13. *What visual aids, if any, will best enhance this presentation?* There are several determining factors: the message, size of the room and audience, seating arrangements, your topic, the amount of time you have to speak, and equipment available. You will learn in chapter 7 the ins and outs of making and handling visual aids and how to select the right one for your presentation.

14. *What equipment will I need and what is available?* You already know if you'll have a lectern and sound system, but you also need to know if you'll have support equipment such as an overhead or 35 mm projector and a viewing screen. Will a flip chart or chalkboard be available? If nothing is available for your use and you don't have equipment of your own, you may have to restructure your speech without visual aids.

Plan ahead to have someone help you carry your visual aids and equipment, or get a pushcart or luggage carrier to transport them.

15. *How much time do I have to speak?* Have you ever sat through a speech and wished you could turn off the speaker? Some speakers don't need a watch to time their speeches, they need a calendar. It was Thomas Edison who said that God made the talking machine, but he—Edison—made the first one that could be turned off.

It's important to stay within the suggested time limits set by the program coordinator. Many meetings have time constraints because people have to get back to work, another event is scheduled for the room, or the overall program has a specific time frame. Running overtime is not only rude, it's unprofessional. If you run overtime, you may be cutting into another speaker's time, thus forcing that person to do some fancy footwork to make last-minute changes in her presentation. I know that feeling. Been there. Done that. Wasn't happy.

If you're asked to speak for fifteen minutes, *do not* speak for forty-five. Your audience will begin squirming in their seats, wondering if and when you'll stop talking. If you're asked to speak for an hour and speak for only twenty minutes, your audience may feel cheated, especially if they paid to hear an hour's worth of information. If you don't know how long you're expected to speak, *ask* and then stay within that time frame.

16. *What time should I arrive?* Early. Arrive early enough to get a feel for the environment, to check your equipment, to get a sense of the audience's energy, and to relax. Talk with your audience before your speech. Build rapport before you get to the lectern. Of course, this is not always possible, but it sure helps lessen the nervousness if you can do so.

If you're to speak away from home and you arrive at your destination the night before, if possible, arrange to have access to the speaking room so you can set up all the necessary tools and rehearse one last time. It isn't necessary to run through your entire presentation, but do enough of it to feel comfortable in the room and assure yourself that everything is going to work as it should.

17. *How far is the location from my home?* If you're speaking at a service club in your hometown, you probably know the building's location and how long it takes to drive there. If the speaking location is new to you, make a dry run at the same time of day you'd leave for the actual speaking engagement. Allow extra time for traffic, detours, and delays. Know where to park or if there's valet parking. It's always better to arrive early and wait than to arrive late and have to rush getting set up.

If you must travel a long distance, you'll need to know what travel arrangements have been made and who is paying for them. This would also be a good time to pin down travel and hotel expenses, too. If you are representing your company, these arrangements are usually taken care of for you—but never assume that this is so.

18. *Will people be eating or drinking while I'm speaking?* The rattling of dishes and clanging of glasses and silverware as servers move about can be a distraction to you and to those trying to listen to you. If possible, request that you speak after the meal is finished, but if that's not possible, plan for the worst.

You can bet that if the audience has been drinking before or during your presentation they will be talkative and some people will be argumentative. Personally, I stay clear of this situation. I decline any speaking engagement where there will be a lot of heavy drinking. It just doesn't pay to put myself into a lose-lose situation.

19. *Will there be other activities going on nearby?* Will there be a concurrent workshop session going on in the next room with a speaker using the king of all microphones? How about a wedding with loud music, or a pep rally for a national sales organization? It is difficult to overcome these horrific distractions, but you can plan around them. Ask if it's possible to change the room. Would using a microphone help? By knowing what to expect, you might be able to work something out with your contact person or the management of the hotel or restaurant.

20. *Will there be other speakers?* What is their subject? If you are part of a program with other speakers, you need to know what they'll be talking about. Find out what their topics are. Listen and pay close attention to the speaker before you, so you can refer to or build on his or her material, making your speech stronger and more entertaining.

Lucy Stone, an activist for women's rights and temperance, once spoke after P. T. Barnum, who had just delivered a humorous rendition of a drunk. She said, "I feel, after the treat we have had from our friend Barnum, that you may not find so tasteful the sober facts which I intend to speak about. I could not help thinking, when my friend Barnum was speaking of the drunkard, that while we could laugh at the picture, should that man have been our brother, father or son, we should feel the deepest pity and the deepest grief." (*The Toastmaster,* April 1992).

What if the previous speaker uses "your" jokes? Should you go ahead and repeat them? My advice is, no. It will take some fast work to adjust at the last minute, but do it. Your joke, unless you can rework it, will fall flat, making you look foolish.

21. *When will I be speaking—morning, afternoon, or evening?* If you're speaking at an all-day conference, are you scheduled to speak after dinner, before lunch, or first thing in the morning—or are you the last speaker following a long line of speak-

ers at the end of the day? Each time of day has its special disadvantages and advantages.

Early morning is not always good, because some people may not be fully awake and may be wandering around, sleepy-eyed and grouchy, trying to find the coffeepot. On the other hand, many people are fresh and full of anticipation of great things early in the morning. The afternoon has its problems with some people getting the "afternoon drags," but other folks come alive in the afternoon.

Being the last speaker of the day is hardest. After people have sat through hours of speeches, they're looking forward to going home, having dinner, or joining the cocktail hour, and it's hard to hold their attention. Some may have left, and you'll find yourself looking out into a room full of empty seats. If you lack confidence, I suggest you beg off speaking in the last position of the lineup.

If you are the after-dinner speaker, you can bet people will want to take a quick break, use the restroom, or grab a smoke.

Also, find out if you're speaking in a concurrent session opposite another speaker who is well known or who has a more popular topic. This has happened to many speakers at conferences. It's a real kick in the ego to find only five or six people in your audience while the next room is filled to capacity. You could ask if your time slot can be changed, or you could go ahead, like a trouper, and give all you have to your small, appreciative audience. You may not have a choice of time slots, but if you do, pick the one best for you, your topic, and your audience.

22. *How will I be introduced?* It's important that you have someone introduce you, so everyone in your audience knows who you are, and why you have come to speak to them. Most important, the introduction builds your credibility.

Never assume that the program coordinator is enthusiastic about speaking, or that she knows how to make an introduction. When asking who will introduce you, don't be surprised if the answer is, "Oh, whoever is available that day." Don't leave this to chance. Pin down the program coordinator and find out who will make your introduction. With all the planning the coordinator has to do, it could be that she never thought about your introduction. Get the name, phone number, and address of the person introducing you. Call him or her and introduce yourself. Write your own introduction and make several copies. Send your introducer a copy. Give one to the publicity coordinator. Carry a copy of your introduction to the event; often the introducer shows up but the written introduction doesn't. Don't let the person "wing it." You have spent too much time on your speech to have it blown off. Hand the introducer the extra copy and emphasize the importance of using your words.

23. *What facilities are available for the comfort and convenience of the audience?* The proximity of restrooms, telephones, coffee machine, water fountain, and coatroom can have a direct bearing on your speech. You can bet if you're speaking to a group of businesspeople, someone in the audience will have a pager and will be called out of the room in the middle of your speech, missing a portion of your presentation. The longer that person has to search for a telephone, the longer it will take her to get back to you. It's a good idea to announce at the beginning of your presentation where the facilities are and when the group can expect a break to use them.

24. *Will I be interviewed by the local media after my speech?* Your topic may be timely and of importance to the local community. Don't be surprised if the media show up to cover the event and to interview the coordinator and the speaker.

25. *How can I gain more speaking experience before I give this speech?* There is no lack of information about how to give a speech. What women lack most is the experience of making a speech. The only way to learn a skill is through practical experience. No amount of reading, listening to audio tapes, or watching videos can substitute for actual experience.

Start with your local community's service clubs and organizations. They are hungry for speakers and will jump at the chance to have you speak to them. Work on a topic that is of interest to you and of importance to the audience. Don't worry about perfection. You'll probably make mistakes, but remember that's okay. This is your training ground. I also suggest joining Toastmasters International. This is an excellent way to practice your speaking skills in a nonthreatening environment and receive helpful feedback on how you can improve.

26. *How much time should I take to prepare and practice?* That's a question only you can answer. Everyone's ability for putting a speech together varies. For some, it can be a matter of days, for others, it takes weeks to prepare, research, write, and rehearse a speech. The more complex the speech, the more time it will take to prepare, but even a short five-minute speech can require weeks of preparation.

Your skill level determines how much time you should give to rehearsal. If you still feel a little shaky after going through your speech eight times, go through it again until you feel comfortable with the material, your visual aids, and your gestures.

There's no time like the present to begin preparing a speech you might make next year. It takes time to gather information and arrange it into a well-prepared speech. You can't do it overnight.

These are a lot of questions to address, and for a very good reason. I don't know about you, but I don't like surprises that jump up and bite me. When I'm speaking and my reputation is on the line, I want to do the best job I can. People pay me for my time, talents, and knowledge; I have an obligation to make sure they get what they pay for. You may not be getting paid for making an announcement or talking about your vacation in South America, but you should feel a sense of responsibility to your audience, or at least to yourself. Take pride in everything you do, and do it well. The old saying, "It's good enough for government work," has become, for some, a way of life. They get by. But as Tom Peters said in *Success*, "Not bad isn't good enough." If getting by is what you want, fine. But just getting by will not cut it for women in today's business world. You must plan that speech, and plan for success.

3

Writing the Speech

*I quote a good deal in my talks . . . I do like to call
upon my radiant cloud of witnesses to back me up,
saying the thing I would say, and saying it so much
more eloquently.*

LEONORA SPEYER, *On the Teaching of Poetry*

Writing a speech is a creative process of stringing words together in a logical order, similar to stringing musical notes together to create a song. As every song has a different melody and mood, every speech has a unique tone, style, and message.

What method is best for writing a speech? The process of writing a speech is different for each individual. Violet Meek, Dean and Director of the Ohio State University at Lima, says many of her speeches are composed on a tape recorder. "The way we write differs from the way we speak. I talk into a tape recorder because the rhythms are different than when writing a speech out on a word processor." She finds that natural phrases such as, "Well now, let's think about it" and "Well, what do you think?" are included where they wouldn't be if she were to sit at her word processor and type. Meek also composes inspirational speeches to music playing in the background. "Never underestimate the power of music to call out the analogy you want to use," she said.

Fiction writers have various methods for developing their ideas into stories. Some use a stream of consciousness. They start writing and let their thoughts flow freely until there aren't any ideas left. Some start in the middle. Others write the last chapter first and fill in the plot as they go along.

The good news is there is no one correct way to write your speech. The bad news is you'll have to discover what works best for you through trial and error.

Where do those ideas come from? Elizabeth Davis, author of *Woman's Intuition*, says her creative thoughts arise while she is running, driving, or dancing.

For me, my most inventive thoughts happen just as I'm falling asleep or waking up. I have spent many nights turning on and off the light on my nightstand to make notes, until my husband complained. A woman in one of my classes told me about her technique of setting a tape recorder by the bed. She used a voice-activated model. Whenever ideas suddenly came, she didn't have to turn the recorder on, she just talked. This sounded like a great idea, so I tried it. When I awoke the next morning I found twenty minutes of uninterrupted snoring. My husband's, of course.

THE BEGINNING—GRAND OPENINGS

Many speeches are like starting a cold car. The key is inserted into the ignition, sending an electrical charge to the starter. The engine spits and sputters, and finally, laboriously turns over. Once running, the engine purrs along to the end of the journey. Many speeches, too, are tough to get started, but once started, they run smoothly. Unfortunately, in the meantime, the riders have decided to get out and walk.

The opening of a speech should be given as much consideration as the rest of the speech—and it should never be boring. Plato said in *The Republic*, "The beginning is the most important part of the work." I'd go a step further by saying that the opening of a speech is *crucial* if you hope to capture the audience's attention. You seldom get a second chance.

The opening of your speech should engage the listener and arouse interest, establish rapport, set the tone of the speech, prepare the audience for what's to come, and build suspense.

The opening must be relevant to the rest of the speech, as it hints at the information to follow. If you start out right, you'll accomplish just that. The audience will wait breathlessly to hear every word you say. Peggy Noonan, who was a speechwriter for former presidents Ronald Reagan and George Bush, says that when you write a speech you must first establish that you are a warm and interesting person. Set out to make the audience lean forward and listen to information that is interesting and valuable.

The opening has four parts. Each element requires careful planning.

The Greeting

The first part of the opening should come easily, because it is something you say every day: "Hello" or "Good morning." The greeting need not be lengthy, with an acknowledgment of every prominent person in the audience or recognition of all dignitaries seated at the head table. Garry Trudeau, the cartoonist, once parodied the kind of "all-inclusive" greeting that often opens a political speech when he began a talk at Yale University:

Dean Kagan, distinguished faculty, parents, friends, graduating seniors, Secret Service, class agents, people of class, people of color, colorful people, people of height, the vertically constrained, people of hair, the differently coiffed, the optically challenged, the temporarily sighted, the insightful, the out of sight, the out-of-towners, the Eurocentrics, the Afrocentrics, the Afrocentrics with Eurailpasses, the eccentrically inclined, the sexually disinclined, people of sex, sexy people, sexist pigs, animal companions, friends of earth, friends of the boss, the temporarily employed, the differently employed, the differently optioned, people with options, people with stock options, the divestiturists, the deconstructionist, the home constructionist, the homeboys, the homeless, the temporarily housed at home, and God save us, the permanently housed at home.... (Reprinted from *Editor's Workshop*, December 1991).

The greeting is also the time to thank your introducer. "Thank you for that wonderful introduction" is always appropriate—the audience will never know that you wrote your own introduction.

Use your greeting to get the audience involved right away. When you say good morning to your audience, you'll seldom get a huge response, but if you repeat "Good morning" louder and with more emphasis, the audience will get the message that they should respond in kind. Once you've made contact with them, they'll feel part of your presentation.

The Attention Grabber

The beginning of your speech must reach out and grab your listeners, shaking them, compelling them to listen. The type of attention grabber you choose depends on several factors: the type of speech being made, the audience, the topic, the speaking situation, your personal delivery style, and, most of all, what feels comfortable.

You may want to prepare the attention grabber last. Choosing one may be difficult until you have developed the body of the message. You won't know which type of grabber will work best. Once you know what approach you will take, select one of the following twenty-two types of attention grabbers that work well with your message.

1. *Make a startling statement.* For example, while unfolding a piece of paper, say, "Ladies and gentlemen, I have just been handed a note. It reads, tomorrow has been canceled," for a speech about environmental pollution.

2. *Ask a rhetorical question.* With a rhetorical question, you don't expect an answer. You're getting the audience mentally involved, making them ponder your question. "What would you

do if you knew someone was breaking into your home at this very moment?" could launch a speech about breaking and entering by computer hacks.

3. *Ask for a show of hands.* Get people physically involved. When asking for a show of hands, raise your hand in a prompting gesture to encourage the audience to follow your lead. If your listeners know they are expected to respond, they will pay attention.

4. *Use an appropriate, well-known quotation, poem, or saying.* Quotations enhance your credibility and authority. Use quotes having the same tone as your speech, and fit quotes by famous leaders, thinkers, writers, and humorists to your topic.

Mary Boykin Chesnut said during the Civil War, "Woe to those who began this war if they were not in bitter earnest." This quote might work for a speech about commitment. Almost any quote from Erma Bombeck is a great opening for a humorous speech about the daily life of a housewife, a mother, or even today's busy woman executive. The first few words of the Pledge of Allegiance would be an appropriate opening for a patriotic speech.

Quotes are easy to find—the shelves of your local library are full of quotation books—but a word of caution. Many quotes have been repeated to the point of becoming clichés. Find new material. Most newspapers use quotes as fillers. Start clipping and saving them.

When using a quote, always give credit to the originator.

5. *Tell stories.* Stories relate information and make your point more interesting than cold, hard facts. With a story, you pull the audience into your speech as they visualize the scenes you describe.

There are several types of stories that work well for openings. A moralistic story makes the audience feel good. A mystery builds suspense and intrigue. People love a good mystery told with a dramatic flair. A sad story gets the audience emotionally involved as it tugs at their heart. Personalize your story. Audiences relate to real people with real experiences. Relating personal experiences adds color and interest to your opening, it also adds a note of authenticity. It shows that you are involved in your topic and that you speak from experience.

6. *Use humor.* We love to laugh; we need to laugh. Funny stories tickle us, make us chuckle, giggle, or even let out a hearty belly laugh. Humor builds rapport and sets the tone for your speech by telling the audience they're going to have a good time. Beginning with humor will put your listeners in a receptive mood.

However, don't start by saying, "Before I begin, I'm going to tell you a joke." Opening a speech with a "straight joke" takes a special talent. The timing must be perfect or the joke will die. If you bomb right at the beginning of your speech, you'll have a hard time regaining the confidence of your audience.

7. *Let the audience in on a personal tidbit.* The easiest way to build rapport with the audience is to reveal something about yourself that says you're human.

I remember when Barbra Streisand told an Academy Awards audience how she had just gotten a run in her nylons. Every woman who has ever gotten a run in her stockings at the most important moment in her life understands how she felt.

8. *Show a visual aid.* An unusual object will get the audience wondering why you're displaying it and what it has to do with your speech. Wave a wad of money around and ask the audience if they would like some of it.

9. *Refer to the audience.* Compliment the audience or the group leader on a recent achievement or award. Mentioning their contribution shows you're interested in them and took time to find found out what they do.

10. *Talk about the occasion.* Mention the number of candles on the cake at a birthday celebration and comment that the fire department is standing by.

11. *Comment on the location.* I once spoke at a local country club that overlooked a well-manicured golf course. Looking out over the lush grass, I said, "I wanted to play golf once, but that was before I discovered that playing golf involved a lot of walking interrupted by foul tempers, bad arithmetic, and a lot

of people in funny clothes." Every golfer in the room knew what I meant.

If you are visiting from another city and if you truly feel the city would be a nice place to live, compliment the town, its buildings, parks, or roads.

12. *Recall a recent or well-known local event.* Read the newspaper. Find out what's been going on that ties into your topic. "I see that your local little league won the state championship" would be a good opening for a speech about team sports, community-supported activities, or sports-related injuries.

13. *Refer to the weather, the time of year, or a holiday.* January of 1994 was not what I call pleasant, with frigid temperatures dipping below freezing for days, canceling school, business meetings, and social affairs. One of my workshops fell victim to the minus-ten-degree temperatures. When the weather finally warmed and the rescheduled session met, I opened with: "I'm happy to see you survived the icy cold weather and are here this evening without having to plow your way out of your driveways or through the parking lot."

The seasons of the year make interesting openings. Each has a significant influence on us. Spring makes us feel young again; fall gives us a sense of well-being; summer bubbles with activity; and winter provides a time for rest. Relate the origins of April Fools Day or All Saints Day.

14. *Speak in a foreign language.* If your audience is mainly English speaking, beginning with a phrase or sentence in a foreign language will heighten interest, and intrigue the audience. Just make sure you provide a translation.

15. *Paint a memorable scene in the mind of the audience.*

When I was a small child growing up in Nebraska, my family and I lived on a twenty-acre farm where we raised chickens, hogs, a few head of cattle, a goat for milk, and a horse we kids called Jollup. We had fresh vegetables from the garden, milk from the cows, and pork from the pigs. Every Saturday morning the smell of homemade bread floated through the house, and four hungry, barefoot kids raced to the kitchen for a warm slice. About the only thing we ever ate from a store was the candy my father brought home once a month from town.

I can't recall the speaker's name, but the vision remains.

16. *Recall a national or world event.* Check history books and newspapers for a story that relates to your topic, and work it into your opening.

17. *Establish a common ground with the audience.* As I arrived to speak to a service organization, several people approached me and asked if I came from Texas. They had read the announcement in their newsletter saying I had graduated from the University of Texas. They were from Texas and wanted to share the Texas experience. (Texans do that sort of thing.) I quickly fit that newly acquired information into my opening and established a common bond with the audience, building rapport.

If you belong to another chapter of the same organization you're speaking to, mention this and how your chapter is similar.

18. *Solicit a unified agreement from the audience.* "There are just too many laws today, with too many people telling us how to live, what to do, and how to do it. We need to get ourselves organized and fight against lawmakers who intrude on our basic freedoms," could be the opening for a speech about government regulations.

19. *Give a definition.* If your subject is one that is new or unfamiliar to the audience, beginning with a definition not only builds interest in your subject, but introduces information. For example, "Pantheism: a doctrine that equates God with the forces and laws of the universe." Then go on to talk about the creation theories or myths, and how they apply in today's world.

20. *Use sound effects.* Talking about wild animals? Open with a lion's roar or strange bird call. Talking about sports? Try blowing a referee's whistle and signal for "time out."

21. *Read an interesting, but short, article or headline from a newspaper.* An unusual obituary or a column like that of Chuck Shepherd, a syndicated columnist who writes "News of the Weird," draws interest.

22. *Try a novelty approach.* Bouncing a beach ball and throwing it over the heads of the audience is a fun way to begin a speech about your summer vacation. Break open a fortune cookie with a saying that just coincidentally reads, "The beginning of wisdom is to desire it" for your speech about education. Talk like an auctioneer trying to sell an idea or opportunity. If you have a good singing voice and the courage, try singing a jingle or song.

Deliver the novelty opening with a dramatic flair. The more overstated the opening, the better. Yell, scream, get silly if you choose. I once saw a woman run up to the lectern, sniff the air, and yell, *"What's that smell?"* to begin her speech about the condition of her teenage son's tennis shoes after summer camp.

Not all of these attention grabbers will work for you, and not all will be appropriate for the audience, the occasion, or your topic. No single type of grabber is better than any of the others. Thoughtfully choose the right one for each speech.

The Overview

By giving an overview, you prepare the audience for what is to come. This doesn't have to be complicated. It can be as simple as, "Today we are going to look at possible solutions for preventing ..." or "I will discuss three ways to improve ..." You're summarizing the main points ahead of time, so the audience knows what to expect. The overview should not be confused with your purpose statement, however.

The Purpose Statement

The purpose statement explains your reasons for speaking. It tells the audience what they should do with the information you are about to give them. Are they to take action or to analyze a problem or important issue, or do you simply wish to entertain them? It alerts them to the benefits they'll receive by listening to you.

The audience found your speech about bluebirds entertaining, but did they know they were supposed to vote for the special tax that would provide funds for a bird sanctuary? If your purpose is clearly stated at the beginning of your speech, the audience will hear the message you intend them to receive.

Such phrases as, "Today, I want you to consider . . ." or "This information will give you a better understanding of . . ." or "I will show you how you can take action . . ." guide the audience in the direction you want them to take.

When I am speaking about how to control nervousness, my overview and purpose statement goes something like this: "Today I am going to show you three ways you can learn to control those butterflies that take up residence in your stomach, so that you can become more confident speaking before an audience."

Fully define your purpose, then write your purpose statement at the top of the page. Refer to that purpose statement often to help you stay on track and focused while writing the rest of the speech. Ask yourself from time to time, "Does what I've written address my purpose or have I strayed from the point?"

Other things to consider about your opening are:

• Don't tell the audience that it's nice to be here. Show them. Be upbeat, smile, and show that you're enjoying yourself.

• Don't open with an apology for any part of your speech, your lack of preparation, or the poor quality of your visual aids. You won't have to tell them you aren't prepared; they'll know soon enough.

• Don't tell them you're nervous. They probably won't notice unless you draw it to their attention.

• Don't begin your speech with, "The title of my speech is . . ." This reminds me of children in elementary school as they recite a story they have written. Don't ask if everyone can hear you. You should have worked that out before you began.

• Deliver the opening with enthusiasm. A startling statement will fall flat if delivered in a monotone voice or while fumbling with your notes. A story opening requires a dramatic delivery with exaggerated hand gestures and facial expressions. If you look and sound interesting, the audience will look forward to hearing the rest of your speech.

You are now ready to move on to the body of your speech by making a smooth, unobtrusive transition.

TRANSITIONS—CEMENTING THE SPEECH TOGETHER

Use transitions to make sure your audience knows where you're headed, when you've shifted gears, and when you're drawing to the conclusion of your speech. Transitions are like the subheads in magazines, letting the reader know something new is coming. As a bridge links one island to another, transitions keep the audience moving along with you by linking one thought to another.

Transitions are easy to use, and there are many to choose from. Here are just a few:

> *when introducing an example:* for example, for instance.
>
> *when giving additional information:* again, also, and, furthermore, in addition, moreover, too, incidentally, another fact to consider.
>
> *to compare and/or contrast:* in contrast, but, in the same manner, similarly, however, rather, instead, nevertheless, on the other hand, on the contrary, looking at it another way, whereas.
>
> *to emphasize a point:* above all, even more, I repeat, in fact, indeed, let me say again, let's direct our attention to.
>
> *to clarify:* in other words, let's look at this another way, in different terms.
>
> *to enumerate:* first, further, second, finally.
>
> *to state similarities:* by the same token, in like manner, likewise.
>
> *as an aside:* by the way, coming back to, incidentally, to digress, let me shift gears for a moment, that reminds me.
>
> *to show results:* as a result, consequently, so, then, therefore, as you can see.
>
> *as a time reference:* afterward, at last, at the same time, eventually, formerly, in the meantime, now, previously, since then, moving to the second part, up to this point.
>
> *leading to the conclusion:* in conclusion, in short, we now see, to summarize, to sum up, for these reasons, in brief, in ret-

rospect, what it all adds up to, let me say in closing, let me leave you with this thought.

THE MIDDLE—BUILDING THE STRUCTURE

The middle of a speech is the heart of your message, and should enlighten, encompass, and enthuse the listener. This is where all the information you have gathered starts to take shape and fulfill your purpose. No matter what your topic or purpose, your message will be more clear and more understandable if you follow a set organizational structure.

The simplest structure for me is one I learned in high school. Write down three points you feel are the most important. For example, a speech about caring for your dog could encompass the three major areas of grooming, shelter, and nutrition. Most short speeches of fifteen to twenty minutes should cover two, maybe three, but no more than four points. There are exceptions to this, of course, but a twenty-minute speech usually cannot include more than that amount of information.

Next, put your major points in an order you feel makes sense. Should feeding come first or should grooming? Maybe shelter is more important. Does it matter? Go through and make a topical statement about each major point. For example, first point: "Your dog should have sufficient shelter to protect it from the cold in winter and the heat in summer." Second point: "Good nutrition doesn't have to be costly" or "A shiny coat can be accomplished by a good diet." Third point: "What you should know before taking your dog to the groomers."

Note: Each of these major points could be a basis for a separate speech.

Using all the information you have in your head and the additional information you have collected through research, write down everything you can think of about your first point—shelter. Do this for each major point. Fill in with definitions, appropriate quotes, illustrations, and advice from experts to support your claims. Don't worry about it being perfect, just write. Editing comes later.

Look at organizing information as an inverted triangle. The top is broad, encompassing the overall topic. As the triangle narrows, the topic begins to come into focus and becomes more specific. You must decide on how to narrow the topic to: (1) fit the time constraints, (2) suit the audience's needs, and (3) fulfill your purpose.

Let's use photography as an example. Photography is too broad a subject to cover in a brief speech, even an hour-long one. Narrow the focus. How about photographic lighting? Continue narrowing. What influence does lighting have on a picture? How does lighting add strength to a picture? How does it affect the contrast of the photograph, and how does it set a specific mood? Now you're getting somewhere.

The inverted structure of a speech about photography might look like this:

Broad Topic—Photography
General Topic—Lighting
Specific Topic—Effects

The main points of a speech on the effects of photographic lighting would look something like this:

A. First point—Studio Portraits
   1. Topic statement
   2. Support material
B. Second point—Candid Shots
   1. Topic statement
   2. Support material
C. Third point—Outdoor Portraits
   1. Topic statement
   2. Support material

Each topic statement *must* be backed by support material. Your support material should always prove or clarify your message through specific examples, personal experience, graphics,

statistics, testimony, and/or quotes. Look at each main point as
a mini speech. If you take point B out of the speech will the
rest of the speech still make sense? Will point B make sense by
itself? It should.

ORGANIZATIONAL PATTERNS
THAT KEEP YOU ON TRACK

Women are natural organizers. We organize social and business
events, coordinate family outings, plan vacations and meetings,
and develop weekly menus and monthly training programs. Some
of us have changed the face of civilizations. So organizing a
speech should be as easy for us as playing tennis without a net.

A well-organized speech is like a road map to lead your audience from point A to point B. If your information is unorga-
nized, your audience may become lost along the way. Before
you lose your listeners, take a good look at your speech and
ask yourself if it is logical. Is there a pattern the audience can
easily follow, or will they become confused, give up in frustration, and stop listening?

Basic patterns for organizing information into a logical order
are:

1. Cause and Effect or Effect and Cause

The cause-effect pattern is used when you want to describe a
situation (the cause) and its results or consequences (the effects).
For example, you recognize potholes as a potential hazard. Uti-
lizing the cause-effect pattern, you state that potholes can cause
many problems, such as misaligned tires, traffic accidents, and
costly repair bills.

With the effect-cause method you identify and analyze a problem or a result and trace its cause. If your car seems suddenly
out of alignment, you could trace the cause to potholes.

Use caution when using this pattern, however. It's easy to
identify a single cause for an effect, when several causes need
to be considered. For example, the misaligned tires could be the
result of an unskilled mechanic.

Another example: What effects can fad diets produce? You could say fad diets result in the regaining of weight lost, decline of health, poor eating habits, and higher food cost. However, don't make the mistake of saying that poor eating habits always result from a fad diet. There could be many other causes.

2. Chronological

Perhaps the most useful, simplest, and easiest pattern to use is the time sequence. Use this pattern when you want to explain events in relationship to time, such as giving instructions for performing a task; explaining what comes first, next, then last; when moving from new to old; establishing then and now; or creating a sequence of day, month, and year.

Instructions for a recipe are given in a step-by-step method: first, preheat oven; second, mix dry ingredients; third, blend in remaining ingredients, et cetera. Instructions for putting a toy together say to follow step one, step two, and so on.

When giving historical background, we view history in a chronological order from the past to the present, and sometimes beyond to the future. To demonstrate how your service club or organization has or hasn't met its goals, you might start with (past) information about how and on what principles the club was founded; continue with what your club is or is not doing to continue those ideals (present); and then tell what your club could do to reach its goals (future).

3. Compare and Contrast

Compare the similarities between two things or contrast them by showing how they differ. Compare how one city manages its waste disposal with another city's program. Show the relationship between crime in the city with that in rural areas. Make a comparative evaluation. For example, you may be asked to contrast the various qualities of two computers under consideration for purchase. Your criteria for the evaluation could include the ease of operation, cost, compatibility, available service, and durability.

Contrasting is done by stating the differences between similar things. For example, demonstrate differences by contrasting the good with the bad, practical with impractical, advantages with disadvantages.

You can also contrast by showing the pros and cons of an issue. Show both sides of the argument or take one side of the issue. Demonstrate the positive qualities of each, then the negative. Depending on the type of speech you're making, you may or may not be required to draw conclusions.

4. Problem / Solution

What do you do when you have a problem? You find ways to solve it. It sounds simple enough, and it is, if you follow these steps:

• Identify the problem clearly and accurately—something is unsatisfactory, deviates from the norm, or needs correcting. A problem could be lack of sales, personality conflicts within the office, the rise in crime rate, or deciding where to have the annual Christmas party.

• Explain why the problem is important by presenting statistics to back your claim, show what harm has been done because of the problem, and how that harm impacts the audience.

• Analyze the problem. There could be many causes for the problem; explore the possibilities.

• List possible solutions. Offer solutions such as better drug-enforcement training of police officers, more police on night patrol, or better education of citizens on how to protect their property.

• Select the best solution.

• Consider both negative and positive consequences of the solution. To be fair, you must present both sides.

• Tell why your solution is the best at this time. Be prepared for objections. Offer information on how your solution has been successful in other situations.

• Put the solution into action.

5. Motivational Sequence

This pattern, developed by Dr. Alan H. Monroe, has five steps and has been used as a persuasive model for college students. You'll notice a similarity to the problem-solving pattern, but the names of the steps are different.

- Attention   Call attention to the problem. State clearly what problem exists.
- Need   Show that a need for change exists or that a problem needs to be solved.
- Satisfaction   Present your solution to the problem presented in the first step.
- Visualization   Show what life would be like with and without your solution.
- Action   Give the audience a plan of action so they can help solve the problem.

The motivational sequence can be used for almost any situation in which you want to persuade an audience to buy a product, change a belief or attitude, support your efforts and ideas, or do something you want.

6. Spatial

Describe a setting or layout such as a room, an office, or a building by using the spatial pattern. Don't jump around. Establish a logical pattern and stay with it. Pretend you are a realtor describing a house. You can begin with the outside and work toward the inside. Once inside, describe the ceiling, the walls, then the floor. Take the audience from room to room, from one floor to another. Then talk about the furnishings by starting at one end of a room and going room by room. The idea is to create a vivid image in the minds of your audience helping them visualize the space being described.

There are two sub-patterns within the spatial pattern:

- Geographical: Use a geographical pattern when you're discussing places on the map—east to west, north to south, et cetera. An example would be grouping various cities by their region: for instance, Bangor, Boston, and New Haven are in New England while Albuquerque, Phoenix, and El Paso are in the Southwest. Even the planets can be organized by their relationship to the sun within the solar system.

- Directional: Here you describe information in a linear way, front to back, left to right, here to there, up to down.

7. Topical

With the topical pattern, group ideas together by general classification. For example, to describe the traits of a team, you might talk about selflessness, cooperation, camaraderie, and communication. As the public relations director in your town, you would give a glowing report of the school system, religious congregations, service groups, hospitals, library, fire and police departments, and so on. In a discussion on the qualities of a specific automobile model, you would mention its performance, style, safety features, and cost.

History often is taught in chronological order, but it also can be presented topically, through the discussion of the economical, educational, religious, political, and social aspects of a particular period. This book follows a topical pattern.

Other ways to organize information into patterns:

- Alphabetical: By using the first letter of each point, you can set up a system that's easy to follow and remember.

Go one step farther and form an acronym from the initials of the main points. This is a useful trick that helps you as well as your audience to focus on your topic. For example, perhaps you're discussing pollution of the environment, and you want to show how pollutants foul the air, water, and soil. By arranging these three points as water, air, and soil, you form the word *WAS*. Then you can take advantage of the past tense to talk about how the earth could become an extinct planet if we continue to pollute.

- Sequential: All objects and events can be placed in a sequence of some kind. You may organize your message by going from one reference point to another, such as smallest to largest, simplest to most complex, or cheapest to most expensive.

- Numerical: This method works when quoting statistics or numbers. Perhaps you are discussing the crime rate, actuaries, budgets, et cetera. Is the number you want to emphasize high or low? Which figure is more important? You have several options. You may begin with the lowest and build to the highest, or vice versa. You could also use one order in the body of your speech and summarize in the reverse order. The audience will remember longest what they see and hear last.

- Characteristics: Present information by describing characteristics. For example, an Olympic champion is self-disciplined, committed to excellence, and a team player. New mothers are caring, protective, and sleepless.

- Systems: If you're building a talk around the systems of a house, you would discuss the electrical, plumbing, security, heating, and cooling systems. In a speech about the systems of a car, you would discuss the ignition, fuel, exhaust, and cooling systems, and so forth. Likewise, the systems of the human body would include the muscular, nervous, skeletal, and circulatory systems.

- Structure: This pattern is similar to systems in that it relates to things within the subject matter. If, for example, you want to talk about the structure of a house, you could talk about the foundation, framework, windows, floor, and roof. Inside this pattern you also could use the spatial or directional pattern as you talk about the structure of the house from roof to basement.

- Importance: This pattern is purely subjective. What is important to you may not be important to someone else. You determine what is important and assign a significance to it. If you're discussing a possible tax increase in the city's budget to provide funds for better roads and police protection, your emphasis will be determined by whether your audience is the city council or the taxpayer.

Sometimes the level of importance is based on what the audience deems important or interesting. It's purely psychological. A city park will mean different things to different people. Some would say the value of the park lies in preserving nature, while others would consider wildlife education for young people to be more important.

If you want to emphasize one point as more important than others, present that point last, building to the important issue you wish to stress. For example: a) weaker point; b) weak point; c) strongest point.

• Random: Perhaps you don't want to make distinctions. You don't want to draw special attention to one particular person, race, sex, religion, political party, or nationality, or to suggest any one is more important than another. Arrange the listing in such a manner that you don't show a significance.

You may already have discovered that several organizational patterns can be used for one topic. You'll have to decide which works best for your topic. Whichever you choose, remember to break the information down into its simplest form. The whole idea of organizing information is to help your audience understand and remember what you say.

THE END—CONCRETE CONCLUSIONS

The conclusion is where you wrap up your message, bringing your speech to a close. It's the end of the ride—the coda, the finale, the payoff, the last word.

Conclusions aren't always as easy as they may seem. The conclusion, for some women, is the most difficult part of giving a speech. Many speakers just don't know how to bring a speech to a close, so they go on and on. Others don't seem to know what to say to end their speech, so they mutter something like, "Well, that's all I have to say. Thanks for listening to me," and quickly sit down. Neither of these endings is effective.

The conclusion should concisely tie everything together. It should produce results and leave no doubt what you want the audience to do with the information you have given them. It should also unify the audience in support of your cause.

Wrap up the conclusion with as few words as possible. The end of your speech is not the place to add additional information you may have forgotten to mention earlier. I once heard a speaker say, "And now in conclusion . . ." and then go on for another fifteen minutes adding information. The title of her speech? "A Never-Ending Love."

Just as there are many ways to begin a speech, there are several methods to bring your speech to a graceful close. Start with a transitional phrase to let your audience know that you're finishing, then use one of the following conclusions:

1. *Briefly summarize your main points.* If your speech was to inform the audience about health care for the elderly, simply review the main points you covered.

2. *Enlist action from the audience* (always used in persuasive speeches and sales presentations). When you are attempting to persuade, show the audience how they can implement your proposal. Restate the advantages of your proposal, then tell them where, when, and how they can take action by writing to their congressman, signing a petition, voting, buying a product, or accepting an idea or concept. Make it easy for the members of the audience. Put the paper in their hands. Give them the name, address, and phone number of the person you want them to contact. Pass around the petition to be signed.

3. *Tell a story.* Finish with a story the audience will remember and retell the next day.

4. *Use an illustration that emphasizes the central theme of your message.*

5. *Uplift the audience with an inspirational message.* End on a high note. A poem or quote works well here. Recite your poem or quote to recorded music for a more dramatic mood. An inspirational speech should leave your audience wanting more. Finish forcefully and confidently.

6. *Refer back to your opening.* If you began with a story of how you learned to ride a bike, refer to those opening remarks and tie everything together in a nice, neat package.

7. *Look to the future with optimism.* Leave the audience with a philosophic message that gives them hope.

8. *Ask a strong rhetorical question.* "So, what will you be doing five years from today?"

9. *Predict the future.* "If we don't do something now, in another year we won't be able to . . ."

10. *Close with humor.* Leave 'em laughing. An entertaining speech should close as it opened, with humor.

Never close by saying "thank you" to your audience. *What?!* I know this may sound strange. After all, we were taught to be polite, to say "please," "thank you," and "you're welcome." It seems to be just plain good manners to say "thank you" to your audience—but is it effective? Saying thank you to an audience when you were invited to speak sounds apologetic. It's as if you are saying, "Oh, thank you for listening to me. Thank you for staying and not walking out in the middle of my speech."

Think of it this way. When you are asked to speak, you're the one who has taken the time to gather information, write the speech, and practice it. You're the one giving your time to the audience. *They* should thank *you* for all that hard work.

On the other hand, if *you* have asked the audience to gather to listen to your sales pitch, for example, letting them know you appreciate their attention is appropriate. *They* are the ones who have taken time out of their busy schedule to listen to you, so you thank them. Still, avoid the unadorned "thank you." It's more effective to say something like, "I want to thank you for giving me the opportunity to speak to you today on behalf of Hope for Tomorrow."

When giving an inspirational or motivational speech, you will want to leave the audience on an emotional high, with a lump in the throat and a tear in the eye. Professional speakers know the effects of a strong, powerful close. They lift the audience to a natural high filled with emotion.

Leave your audience feeling good. Let the last words of your message ring in their ears as you quietly leave the lectern.

Don't let your powerful ending sag by saying the anticlimactic "thank you."

What should you say? Nothing more.

OUTLINING VERSUS WRITING OUT THE ENTIRE SPEECH

For some women, a quick reference to a brief outline on three-by-five index cards is sufficient to recall what comes next in their speech. Other women only feel comfortable with an entire manuscript in front of them. There are pros and cons to both methods.

Small, unobtrusive cards are the recommended format for notes. They can be kept in a pocket, and held in the palm of your hand for quick reference during your delivery, should a memory lapse occur. Although using index cards is less cumbersome than using larger sheets of paper, they may not always provide enough room for all the information needed. Looking at a few key words or phrases on note cards sometimes can't help you remember the more complex details, definitions, stories, long quotes, joke punch lines, et cetera.

Writing out the entire speech lets you see all your words, but it also tends to cause you to rely on the words and to read them instead of talking them. Your ultimate goal is to sound as if you are talking to your audience in a conversational manner. Another disadvantage of a large sheet of paper is that, if not handled well, the paper becomes a distraction.

Margaret Thatcher, former British prime minister, writes her speeches in longhand, then revises and rewrites them onto small note cards. She memorizes all her speeches, but uses note cards as a safeguard (*The Toastmaster*, December 1992).

You'll have to discover which method works best for you, your delivery style, and your ability to remember large amounts of information. If you are going to use note cards, I recommend that you write out your speech first, before condensing it onto the cards. There are three reasons for this suggestion.

First, this process allows you to see your thoughts more clearly. You will be able to revise and edit, choosing more powerful words. Second, as you become more specific about what you want to say, begin outlining the major points into topical words, then put them onto note cards to be used as memory joggers during the delivery. Finally, key words or phrases on note cards won't help you recall the details in the body of a speech, should you wish to give that same speech again years later.

SUGGESTIONS FOR WRITING NOTE CARDS

After you have written out the entire speech, reduce the written manuscript to note cards by using these suggestions:

1. *Note cards should be no larger than five by seven inches in size.*

2. *Write only the key words or phrases on each card, but avoid making too general a statement.* In the example of photographic lighting, the word *Effects* may not be sufficient to recall specific details of studio, candid, and outdoor lighting.

3. *Write out entire numbers and quotes.*

4. *Use only one side of the card.*

5. *Number each card or page, in case they become scattered.*

6. *Don't staple the cards together.*

7. *If you must use a larger sheet of paper, complete the last sentence on the page.* Don't carry part of it over to the next page or the back side. Flipping the paper can be distracting to the audience. Write only on the top portion of the paper. The farther down you have to look to see the words, the less chance you have to maintain eye contact. Plus, the audience will be looking at the top of your head. Type and double or triple space. If you have a computer, use a large, bold typeface. Also, for easier handling, fold a bottom corner of the paper so you can slide the top page off the next.

8. *Leave room along one side of the card to make notes, and annotate when to use or change slides or use a pause.* This is best done in a colored pen.

9. *Make two copies.* Put one in your briefcase and carry one on your person. You'd be surprised how often notes come up missing the day of the speech.

Remember, notes are to help you. They're not to be used as a crutch. It's better to have them and not use them than to need them and not have them.

Here, in outline form, is an overview of all the elements of a speech. Use it each time you begin to plan a speech on a chosen or assigned topic.

SAMPLE OUTLINE

I. Opening
   A. Greeting
   B. Attention grabber
   C. Overview
   D. Purpose statement
II. Middle—body of main points
   A. Main point
      1. Subpoint
         a) Support material
      2. Subpoint
         a) Support material
      3. Subpoint
         a) Support material
   B. Main point
      1. Subpoint
         a) Support material
      2. Subpoint
         a) Support material
      3. Subpoint
         a) Support material
   C. Main point
      1. Subpoint
         a) Support material
      2. Subpoint
         a) Support material
      3. Subpoint
         a) Support material
III. Closing statement

4

Revising the Speech

*Words, like fashion, disappear and recur throughout
English History, and one generation's phraseology,
while it may seem abominably second-rate to the next,
becomes first-rate to the third.*

VIRGINIA GRAHAM, *Say Please*

You have several pages filled with hundreds of words, but they're only a rough draft. Next comes editing, revising, and cutting. This is where you delete about thirty percent of what took you hours to write. Don't yell. Revising a speech may seem overwhelming at first. That's normal. Most professional writers don't like editing either, but they cut and edit much of what they've written before their manuscripts leave their desk for the mailbox. Poet and essayist Samuel Johnson said, "Read over your compositions, and wherever you meet with a passage which you think is particularly fine, strike it out."

It's difficult to chop away at those wonderfully elegant phrases and words you labored over for days, but it must be done to move your speech forward. It's not my purpose to turn you into a writer, but I would like to give you a few proven guidelines that will help you put your thoughts on paper. Then you can see what you've written; rework the words; and make them more dynamic, interesting, and powerful.

THROUGH THE MAGNIFYING GLASS

"Write, comb it out, rewrite, keep combing," says speechwriter Peggy Noonan. Let's look at your speech closer now. Put that speech under the microscope and see if you can make it stronger, more interesting, and easier to understand by asking the following questions:

1. *Is my purpose clearly stated?* Will the audience understand what I expect them to do with the information?

2. *Is what I've written well organized, with a recognizable opening, body and conclusion, and does the speech have a clear organizational pattern?* Have I used transitions?

3. *Does the speech have a strong central theme that threads throughout the entire speech?* Does my support material contribute to the theme?

4. *Is what I say logical?* Does it make sense?

5. *Is my message specific?* Does everything I say add to my objective, or does it confuse or detract from the topic?

6. *Is my message concise?* Do I get to the point, or do I ramble?

7. *Have I explained my proposal through definition, description, or exposition?* Is every unfamiliar word clearly defined?

8. *Have I used factual information to support my purpose?* And are my facts, names, dates, places, and statistics correct? Are they current? Have I checked every statement for accuracy?

9. *Have I chosen the best information from the best sources?* Are my sources credible?

10. *Have I given attribution to those sources, quotes, and other people's work?*

11. *Is what I say balanced for both sides of the issue, or have I chosen just one side?*

BUILDING YOUR WORD POWER

What you say is the meat of the message; how you say it, the gravy. Words sung softly in a lullaby can lull a baby to sleep.

Words filled with hate and anger can stir a mob to violence. The eloquent words of Winston Churchill sent armies marching into the face of death, while words of encouragement fanned the flames of genius. Powerful words mold the public's mind like a sculptor molds a piece of clay. Any way you use them, words—spoken or written—are a dynamic force.

As you write your speech, remember the audience will hear your words, not see them. So you must write for the ear, not the eye. Select words that help illustrate your meaning and add depth to your speech. Choose words that convey images and paint mental pictures in the minds of the audience, helping them visualize your meaning.

Suggestions for selecting the right words:

1. *Use simple words.* Mark Twain once said, "By hard, honest labor, I've dug all the large words out of my vocabulary."

In other words, forget the hyperbole and overstated. Language does not have to be complicated to be colorful or exciting. You can't go wrong using the KISS method of word choice. *K*eep *I*t *S*imple *S*ister. But remember, your words must be appropriate for the audience, the subject, and the occasion.

Unfamiliar words distract from the meaning of your message. The audience can become confused and miss your message if they have to stop and think about the meaning of a word, and you run the risk of them tuning you out.

Ask yourself, will my audience understand the word *fractious* or will they better understand *irritable* or *quarrelsome?* How about the words *cognizant* or *imbibe?* Can you find simpler words, such as *aware* or *drink?* Why use wordy phrases such as "the recipient affixed his signature to the document," when "he signed the paper" will do? You wouldn't use elevated words when talking with your friends; so why use them in your speech?

A young Benjamin Franklin said to his mother, "I have imbibed an acephalour molluscous." Thinking he had swallowed something poisonous, his mother forced him to take a large dose of an emetic. When he got over the effects of the medicine he said, "I had eaten nothing but an oyster." Then his mother thrashed him for deceiving her. Then and there Benjamin vowed never again to use big words when little words would do (*Principles and Practice of Preaching* by Illion T. Jones).

There may be times when you want to throw in a five-dollar word, however, to build your credibility or to match the educational level of your audience. Just be careful. Make sure you use the word correctly and understand its meaning. If you don't already have one, buy a thesaurus and use it to find a better word choice.

2. *Use words that are concise, specific, and to the point.* Are all the words you use necessary? If not, cut the clutter. For example, "The house located across the street," could be shorten by omitting the word "located." It isn't necessary. Another example, "The maximum age limit for applicants is . . ." Omit the word *"limit."*

3. *Use active voice.* "She placed the overhead slide on the projector," sounds better than, "The overhead slide was placed on the projector by her."

4. *Use vivid, colorful words and phrases that excite the senses.* Give your audience more than words for the ear. Help them to see, smell, taste, and feel your words. Use words such as *trotted, slinked, slithered,* or *strolled* instead of *walked.* Is the car just red or cherry red?

5. *Use power words. Quality, safe, value, free, hope, money, love,* and *profit* are just a few words that satisfy basic human needs.

6. *Choose words that are easy to pronounce.* Can you say *aluminum?* Many people can't. If you stumble over a word or have trouble saying two words together, change them or cut them.

7. *Use your own words, not those of others.* Use phrasings that sound natural to you. We tend to write more formally than we speak, and some phrasing can look fine on paper but sound awkward when spoken. This is where verbalizing your speech becomes important. If you can't say what you wrote comfortably and smoothly, cut it.

TECHNIQUES FOR WRITING A STRONGER SPEECH

1. *Incorporate "you" into the text.* Using the personal pronoun "you" makes the audience feel part of your message. For example, instead of asking "What are the three most important factors in education today?" Rephrase the question to "What do *you* think are the three . . . ?"

2. *Avoid cluttering your speech with too many unnecessary detailed examples or analogies.* If one example explains your point, why go on and on, unless you feel a restatement will make your point clearer? Concise and to the point is the key.

3. *Build questions into your presentation.* Use questions as a device to emphasize key points, to give additional information, gain attention, to encourage participation, and to guarantee understanding.

There are several types of questions. First, ask "close-ended questions" that require only a yes or no or a head nod. "Sam, have you ever gone ice fishing?" or "Carol, would you buy a purple car just because someone said it's the 'in' color this season?" With a close-ended question you aren't soliciting a lengthy answer, you merely want to bring your audience into the speech and hold their attention.

Working within a problem-solving situation you would ask "open-ended questions" that require a more detailed response. For example, "John, what is your suggestion for . . ." or "What was the result of your findings, Marsha?"

Questions pull the audience into your presentation and make them feel special. But be careful. I don't recommend calling on anyone unless you feel sure he or she knows the answer. You never want to embarrass anyone. It's safer to ask for their opinion. "Mary, what do you think about . . ." or "What's your opinion, Bill?" People will offer their opinions more freely in most cases.

Another technique is to ask a "rhetorical question" where you don't expect an answer. Your goal is to get the audience thinking. With a rhetorical question, you don't call on anyone specific. You ask the question to the audience as a whole.

When asking questions, pause and allow the audience time to think about the question. The pause also gives you a chance to take a breath or a sip of water. Ask only one question at a time. When a correct answer is given, make sure you acknowledge the person and praise him or her for their courage in responding.

Building questions into your speech is not the same as asking the audience if they have any questions. We'll look at the Q and A session later.

4. *Get your audience involved.* An ancient philosopher once said, "Tell me, I'll forget. Show me, I'll understand. Get me involved, I'll remember." Don't let your audience remain passive. Get them involved. Ask them to "write this down" or "check your handout." Ask them to turn and look at the person sitting next to them, shake their hand, make funny faces, et cetera, whatever the situation allows.

In my workshops, I like to clarify the difference between a lectern and podium. When the opportunity is right and I use the word *lectern*, I stop and point to the lectern and say, "This is a lectern." I ask everyone to repeat after me, "Lectern." Later, whenever the word *lectern* comes up again. I run over to the lectern, point, and ask, "What's this?" The response will be tiny whispers. I continue doing this throughout my presentation. By the time I'm near the end, all I have to do is point to the lectern and I receive a loud "LECTERN!" in response.

5. *Vary the length of your sentences.* Use short and long sentences to keep your audience's ears from falling asleep. Shorter sentences are easier to comprehend and remember. "We set out for the place where we were going to shop just as the sun began to rise," is too long.

Let's try it again. "We left at dawn for the mall." Keep in mind, however, too many short sentences can create an unpleasant rapid-shot effect if used frequently in succession.

6. *Reinforce your message with repetition.* Use repetition to drive home your message. Dr. Martin Luther King's "I Have a Dream" speech is a perfect example of the use of repetition. He

uses "one hundred years later" four times; "go back" six times; "I have a dream" nine times; and "let freedom ring" ten times.

7. *Rephrase the point.* Because everyone processes information differently, you need to offer many different opportunities for the audience to grasp your meaning. Rephrasing helps the audience retain your message and gives them a chance to catch something they may have missed.

8. *Use physical demonstrations.* My high school history teacher reinforced his message through illustration. To drive home the message about the Peloponnesian War (431–404 B.C.) he placed a chair on top of his desk, sat on it, and pretended to be Lysander as he watched his great navy bring Athens to her knees. What a powerful way to illustrate a dry, dull subject to a group of noninterested high school students! Which high school teacher do you remember? Probably the one who not only challenged you but excited you and made learning fun.

9. *Give examples in series of three.* The Greek philosopher and mathematician Pythagoras said that three is a perfect number. We see evidence to support this all around us. For example: Faith, Hope and Charity; a rag, a bone, and a hank of hair; the Father, Son, and Holy Spirit; and the saying on the Statue of Liberty, "Give me your tired, your poor, your huddled masses."

10. *Arrange sentences so they build to a climax.*
WEAK: "Driving while drinking cost him everything."
STRONG: "Driving while drinking cost him his license, his wife, and finally his life."
WEAK: "Children grow up too fast."
STRONG: "The child grew tall. The child grew strong. The child grew away from home."

11. *Use analogies to explain the unfamiliar.* Author Lilian Rosen uses this example: "The glass in the windshield of your car is a kind of sandwich. Instead of two slices of rye bread, you have two sheets of plate glass. Instead of corned beef or pastrami, you have a thin sheet of plastic vinyl. This glass sandwich is put in a press, heated, and squeezed. The plastic melts a little and binds the sheets of glass together."

12. *Include anecdotes and stories to add interest.* The best anecdotes are stories about real people and events. They can be of famous people, your next-door neighbor, a family member, or about yourself. Tell your story in as few words as possible, using clear, sharp sentences with vivid images. If you can't come up with a real story of your own, Jacob M. Braude's *Complete Speaker's and Toastmaster's Library* (Prentice Hall, 1965) in eight volumes, has many interesting facts, humor, and anecdotes that you can adapt to fit your message.

13. *Use similes.* Words such as *like, as if, is the same as* add sparkle to images. "Her speech was as pointless as an unsharpened pencil." "She has hair as red as paprika."

A good source for similes is *Falser Than a Weeping Crocodile and Other Similes* by Elyse and Mike Sommer (Visible Ink Press, 1991).

14. *Try using a metaphor to make comparisons between dissimilar objects.* "His handshake was a vise." "She is a lamb." Use a variety of metaphors to connect with the audience. One might not be enough to reach everyone.

15. *Include vivid description.* Writers use the phrase "show, don't tell." Vivid descriptions allow the audience to see for themselves what things look, feel, hear, and taste like. If I told you it was a colorful dress, how much do you know about it? But if I told you the dress was a mint green with splashes of yellow, you have a clearer picture that will last a lot longer. "The chair sat beside the table." You see only two things—a chair and a table. But if you say, "A tattered brown chair, barely holding its own weight, leaned against a round, three-legged table," you begin to see another picture.

SPEECH WEAKENERS

1. *Technical phrases and jargon.* Using an alphanumeric message transfer facilitator might be understood by a few techheads, but does anyone else know what it means? Why not call it what it is—a pencil. Technical talk saves time, but only if

everyone understands the meaning of the words being expressed.

When doctors talk to doctors and mechanics talk to mechanics, they'll understand their own terminology. Remember your audience and their profession. What language do they use in their jobs? Will your audience understand computer language? Many adults cringe at the thought of learning to operate a computer, not knowing a ROM from a RAM. Will they understand what a "hot rock discriminator" is and how it works on a metal detector? I said earlier that you must know the educational level and profession of your audience. If not, you'll be met with puzzling stares and soon lose your audience.

The same is true for using foreign phrases, specifically Latin. Some speakers must think that using foreign phrases makes them appear intellectual. Unless everyone understands Latin, don't try to elevate your speech with it. If you do, make sure you interpret the phrase.

2. *Contractions.* Ever sit wondering if the speaker said "can" or "can't"? It's difficult to tell the difference when a speaker runs her words together. If there is a chance the audience will misunderstand you, avoid the contraction and say both words. Plus saying, "it is not fair," has much more impact than saying, "it isn't fair." Saying the words separately allows you to stress the word *not*, adding more emphasis.

3. *Clichés.* One of my first papers in creative writing class as a freshman came back marked, "Don't use clichés." All ten of them were circled in red ink. I didn't understand. How could what I just made up in my head be a cliché? What I had written was "as common as dirt."

Clichés take shortcuts to describe people and things, but have been overused to the point of losing their effectiveness. Using clichés indicates a lack of creativity and makes you and your ideas sound stale and secondhand. Find a new way to express an old idea.

However, clichés give your speech a friendly homespun style. "I am as nervous as a long-tail cat in a room full of rocking chairs," is an old saying that's "as old as the hills," but is effective in expressing an idea. Your personal style, type of speech, and the situation will dictate whether you can get away with using clichés.

4. *Slang.* I have no idea what kids today are talking about. I understand Plato had the same problem. Good means bad, bad means good, cool is hot. If you're talking to a young audience, learn their latest slang, and use it to connect with them. They'll think you're cool, man, or is the word *bad*?

Use business buzzwords in the same manner as technical jargon—sparingly. Today's in words are out tomorrow.

5. *Wordiness.* We live in a fast-paced world. Gone are the days when we could leisurely sit and peruse the morning newspaper while enjoying a cup of coffee. We scan headlines, picking out words and phrases in hopes of gleaning the message, and often skip most of a lengthy story. We have become so accustomed to the high-speed treadmill of life that we listen and hear in much the same manner. We want a fast-paced lesson: Tell me, but make it quick. There is little time for lengthy, unnecessary details cluttered with excessive information.

After you have written your speech, go back and look for those words that don't add to the substance of the message and strike them out.

Also eliminate redundancies such as "old antiques," "9 A.M. in the morning," "original copy," and "join together." While you're at it take a look to see if you have used euphemisms such as they put him "six feet under," she is in the "family way," and he "got the axe." You may want to cut them, too.

6. *Statistics without visuals.* Bob Hope described his physical condition by using statistics. He said, "Today my heart beat 103,000 times; my blood traveled 168,000,000 miles; I breathed 23,000 times; I inhaled 438 cubic feet of air; I spoke 4,800 words, moved 750 major muscles, and exercised 7,000,000 brain cells. I'm tired."

That's a funny story told as only Hope could tell it, but I wonder how many people hearing it could recall the figures moments later. For some people, numbers are difficult to grasp and understand if not shown visually. Tell me a story with one number and I'm content. Use two numbers and I can contrast them. Give me three numbers and I'm confused.

Sure, Hope's purpose wasn't to emphasize numbers; it was purely to entertain, and that's what he did, but could you use numbers in the same way if your purpose was to convey technical information and be successful? Probably not.

If you plan to use statistics, back them up with visual support. Always round out numbers, show their relevance, and then repeat them for clarity and to reinforce their importance. Compare and contrast them to something relevant to show if the numbers quoted are too high or too low. Graphs and charts work best when making comparisons.

7. *Unclear directions.* I play a game in my workshops where we draw pictures to demonstrate how hard it is to give clear directions. It's fun and shows how poorly most of us explain things. I ask the audience to draw a rocking chair. However, I don't say "rocking chair." I ask them to draw a vertical line about four inches long, a two-inch horizontal line about three quarters of the way down the vertical line, and another vertical line downward to match the length of the first vertical line. Then I tell them to draw a semicircle connecting the two vertical lines at the bottom and extend it a half inch beyond the two lines. You would be amazed at how many different versions of a rocking chair I get.

8. *Semantic differences.* Some words have a significance or connotation other than the expressed meaning. For example, to some people the word *cheap* means "low in price." To others, it means "low in quality." *Skinny* and *slender* are perceived differently, too. Tell a friend she looks slender and she'll love you, but tell her she's skinny and she won't.

9. *Overuse of adjectives and adverbs.* Limit the number of modifiers you use. They dilute your effectiveness. Such words as *very, real, too,* and *good* are empty and abstract. If you choose an exciting word in the first place you won't need to give it window dressing.

10. *Abstract ideas.* Using abstract words can place you in jeopardy because they can easily be misunderstood. We view the world in negatives and positives depending on our age and sex and our ethnic, religious, and educational backgrounds. Abstract words such as *love, hate, sin, patriotism, smart,* and *dumb* are interpreted differently and can trigger an emotional response quite different from what we expected. With concrete words such as *desk, automobile,* and *shoe* there is little misunderstanding; we can see, touch, and feel them.

Phrases such as "traditional family values" can be interpreted in different ways, depending on the background of the audience members. You must spell out what you think those values are.

CREATING THE TITLE

The title of your speech is the carnival barker standing on the street corner calling folks to come in and see the show. Oftentimes, the only thing the audience knows about your speech is the title written in a program. Therefore, the title should accurately convey not only the content of your speech, but intrigue and entice the audience to sit and listen to what you have to say. And it should be memorable enough for the audience to recall when they talk about your message the next day. A title can make a shocking statement or state an opinion. It can promise a benefit and set the tone of the speech, whether serious or humorous.

I left creating the title for last because it should be the last thing you do in writing your speech. It's the finishing touch.

Where do you begin finding a title that describes your message? The easiest method is to pull title ideas from within the context of your speech. Find a phrase or several words that best describe what you're talking about. Can you find the title of this book within its pages? It's there on page 78. If that doesn't work, make a trip to the bookstore and check out the titles on the shelves. You'll notice several things about titles: They're catchy and relevant to the content of the book. Take a clue from magazines, movies, and advertisements for additional hints for possible titles.

Most book titles are short. One- or two-word titles don't tell you much about a book, but that doesn't matter. You can pick up a book, scan the pages, read the table of contents, and come away with a pretty good idea of what the book is about. An audience, however, can't pick up your speech and scan it. You need to pack a lot of information into a short title, and that can be difficult. To accomplish this, use a subhead in the title that helps explain the content of the speech. For example, "Dingbats and Other Madness: Creating a Great-Looking Newsletter" uses the word *dingbats* that may not be familiar to many people. But by tagging the word *newsletter* at the end, the audience gets the idea.

Your title should not be so vague that it obscures the topic. A title such as "Communication in the Workplace" is vague and too general, leaving the audience to wonder what part of communication will be discussed. Will the speaker discuss interoffice communications, written communications, telephone etiquette, or communicating between boss and worker? "Making Your Opinions Count" is better, but how about, "Talking to the Boss: Six Ways to Express Your Opinions." Now the audience knows your speech will be about how to communicate your ideas and opinions to the boss.

A few techniques for creating titles are:

• Use humor. "Fishing Just for the Halibut" lets you know the speech is about fishing, but also has a touch of humor with a play on words.

• Offer a benefit. Titles such as "Six Steps to Success," "The Ten Best ...," and "The Joys of ..." give the audience hope that things can be better by following your suggestions.

• Turn a phrase. Take a well-known quote or phrase and twist it. For example, "Venice Anyone?" sounds like "Tennis, Anyone." "Nautical but Nice" is a play on "Naughty but Nice."

• Experiment with alliteration. "Is There a Mouse in Your House?" and "Combat Commuting" are just two examples.

• Build in a mystery to pique curiosity. "The New Silent Killer" has a sense of mystery.

- Turn the title into a question. "Who's Teaching Your Children?"
- Avoid negative assumptions. "Mistakes Women Make in the Office." Sure we all make mistakes, but we don't like having them pointed out. "You'll Never Fail Again." Who said I did in the first place?

The uniqueness of your title can be the deciding factor for whether or not someone wants to spend time listening to you. So put time into its creation.

PART II

Delivery

5

Body Language—
Making the Right Moves

Emotion constantly finds expression in bodily position. . . .

MABEL ELSWORTH TODD, *The Balancing of Forces in the Human Body*

Many women fail to deliver a successful speech because their body language conflicts with their message or doesn't project confidence. Women need to develop skills in using facial expressions, hand gestures, and body movements that are not only powerful, but smooth, well timed, and meaningful to clarify, reinforce, and support their speech.

The way you present yourself to the audience—how you stand, walk, and sit—sends a loud message. Make sure that message is the right one.

A man once told me that body language wasn't important in making a speech. He pointed out that many good stories have been told on the radio where a listener has only the spoken word to form mental images. This is true. Radio dramas of the past brought much enjoyment to millions. But we are talking about making a speech before a live audience—a totally different situation. Those radio performers were professionals, well trained in using their voices to create a desired mood. Whether or not you are a professional speaker, when delivering a speech you need all the help you can get. Using facial expressions, hand gestures, and body movements is the best and least expensive way to enhance that delivery.

Irene Hedrick, a speech training consultant, says that no matter what your words say, unless your gestures are in sync with those words, your listeners will be confused and possibly won't believe you. Words account for about seven percent of a speaker's impact; vocal clues produce thirty-eight percent, and nonverbal communication is responsible for fifty-five percent of what the audience perceives. Your body is a visual aid that helps the audience to understand your message more clearly.

If you don't believe this, try turning off the sound on the TV and watch the action. You'll be surprised how much you can glean by watching the actor's gestures and body movements.

Let's take a look at the three basic elements of body language to better understand why using it correctly is so essential.

EYES—THE WINDOWS TO YOUR SOUL

Shy, girlish, down cast eyes don't make it in today's business world. You must "look 'em in the eye." When you make eye contact with your audience, you make them feel important. It's as if you're saying, "I know you're there. I see you. You are important to me."

Ever talk to someone who wouldn't look at you? Their eyes kept flitting around as if afraid to look at you directly. How did it make you feel? Not making eye contact can be perceived as nervous avoidance or as being insecure and self-conscious. It can also be interpreted as dishonest or crafty. No eye contact could mean you don't care about your audience, making them feel alienated. I once saw a speaker begin his speech with his head down, looking at his notes. He seldom looked out at the audience to acknowledge them. We could have gone on a coffee break and he would never have known.

Looking up at the ceiling or the back of the room, over the heads of your audience, is another way of avoiding eye contact. Please don't do this. They'll sense that you're nervous.

Making eye contact with a small audience is easy. Look at every member of the audience as you speak. Add impact by an occasional nod of the head. It's important to complete a phrase or sentence before looking at the next person. If you move on too quickly, before completing a comment, it might appear as if you aren't interested in that person. Contact is the key word here.

Another important point is not to let your eyes flit around the room selecting only certain individuals. Give everyone the same amount of attention; they're giving you all of theirs. But you don't want to look at any one individual so long or so often that you make them feel uncomfortable. It could appear you're staring at them, sending a wrong signal.

A larger audience requires a different approach. Divide the audience into three sections. Right, left, and center. Look first to your right (or left—doesn't matter) and speak to that section for a few moments. As you shift your eye contact from one side of the room to another, don't just turn your head. Turn your entire body toward that section. To do otherwise will make you appear as if you are giving them only a casual glance.

Not everyone will return your eye contact. Just as it may be hard for you to make eye contact, some people may be uncomfortable looking back at you. They may be shy and avoid your glance. If you see someone look away every time you try to make eye contact, move on. Don't persist.

Do you wear glasses? Glasses tend to hide the eyes, preventing the audience from seeing your expressions. Many speakers wear glasses, and I haven't been distracted unless they fiddled with them. In fact, glasses can help aid in gesturing, if not done too often. Some believe that glasses add sophistication or an educated look. But a word of caution: If you speak in a dimly lighted room at a lectern with a light attached, there may be a reflection on the lens, hiding your eyes.

Eye contact is also critical in the feedback process. You must be able to see your audience's reactions to your message. Are they falling asleep? Do they look confused? You won't know if you don't look at them. We'll talk more about audience feedback in chapter 11.

PUT YOUR BEST FACE FORWARD

The expression on your face reveals your attitude, and should reflect warmth, sincerity, and enthusiasm.

Carol was a good speaker, well organized, and always had something interesting to say, but every time she stepped to the lectern, she pasted a silly grin on her face no matter what the subject. The expression didn't match her movements or gestures; she was sending a mixed message. When asked why she repeatedly made that expression, she said she wasn't aware of it. But after seeing herself on video tape, she discovered her pasted-on smile and realized it was a cover-up for nervousness.

A photographer friend told me you can smile without moving your mouth. Try it. Stand in front of a mirror and hold a piece of paper over your nose and mouth. Now, smile. Watch your eyes. Did they change? Think about that special person in your life. Look closely, you'll see the pupils dilate. Your eyes become large, limpid pools. That's how romance novelists describe a heroine's eyes when she is attracted to a gorgeous hunk.

When you smile, you send a signal to the audience that says, "I'm friendly. I'm having a good time. I'm confident. I like doing this, and I like you." A friendly smile goes a long way in connecting with an audience.

Just as you practiced smiling, practice facial expressions. Stand before a mirror and try producing these positive expressions: sincerity, enthusiasm, happiness, and flirtation. Negative expressions: skepticism, hostility, and confusion.

LET YOUR FINGERS DO THE TALKING

Women need to develop skills in using hand gestures that are smooth, well timed, graceful, and natural to illustrate size and weight, shape, direction, urgency, and degree of importance. Martha Graham said, "The gesture is the thing truly expressive of the individual—as we think so will we act."

Gestures are a natural extension of your message. They say visually what your voice sometimes can't. They dramatize your ideas and stimulate audience participation. They punctuate and emphasize much like an explanation mark and give vitality and authenticity to a speech as they help dissipate nervous tension.

Here's a challenge for you. Hold your hands behind your back and try telling a story. Even with your hands clasped behind your back, I bet your fingers moved. Some people can't express themselves without using their hands to punctuate what they say. They even gesture while talking on the phone.

Gestures should be natural, not choreographed. As you rehearse, watch to see if your gestures are graceful and timed to fit your words. Let your gestures express your feelings. Don't try to force a gesture into your presentation if that gesture feels awkward. It is critically important to find gestures that come naturally and are not stiff, or worse, phony.

Don't fling your arms around in the air just because you feel you should be doing something with your hands. When you aren't using your hands to gesture, find a comfortable position for them or let them hang relaxed by your sides until you are ready to gesture again.

Don't overdo the gestures. Each gesture you make should emphasize a point and have a purpose. Not every word or statement needs to be accentuated. Used too often, gestures become meaningless, placing everything you say on the same level of importance.

Watch pointing your finger. Think how you feel when, as a member of an audience, the speaker points to you and asks a question. You suddenly feel put on the spot. You weren't prepared for this. Should you respond? What do you say? It's better to extend all your fingers outward so no particular member of the audience is being pointed to and made to feel uncomfortable. John F. Kennedy used the finger jab without pointing at anyone in particular.

Gestures should not be exaggerated in such a way that they become a distraction or become comical. The audience is there to hear what you have to say, not to watch a melodrama.

Fit your gestures to the size of the audience—small room, small gestures. A tiny hand gesture easily seen across a table will lose strength fifty feet away in the back of a large auditorium.

In contrast, while speaking in a large banquet hall or auditorium, your gestures need to be large enough for everyone to see.

Although gestures add emphasis and are important to your speech, they shouldn't be so important that they overshadow the content of your message. Focus on what you have to say instead of how you're saying it, because when you concentrate on what you're saying, your speaking style will follow naturally.

Using gestures calls attention to your hands. Soft, supple skin and healthy nails are signs of good hygiene and are important to your overall appearance. Dirty nails and chapped hands scream that you don't take care of yourself. A good manicure with a neutral polish goes a long way in the credibility department.

Types of hand gestures include:

Prompting—Ask for a show of hands by holding up your own hand.

Okay sign—Index finger and thumb forming a circle indicates "just right."

Thumbs up or Thumbs down—Both have a specific meaning. Thumb extended suggests a hitchhiker.

Descriptive—Gestures that show size, height, and weight.

Emphatic—Hands forming a fist show determination.

Stop—Palms facing out, fingers upward with arms extended.

Pleading—Arms extended forward with palms turned up and open.

Who cares? or I don't know—Palms up, fingers pointing outward, and elbows close to your body combined with a shoulder shrug.

POSTURE PERFECT

Your mother wasn't kidding when she told you to stand up straight, walk tall, and sit like a lady. Every woman needs good posture, poise, and grace to command respect. Your body, whether you like it or not, is a visual aid and is the first thing your audience sees before you begin to speak. The way you move, sit, stand, and walk sends a strong message to the audience, so it's important that you take care of your body with a proper diet, the right amount of sleep, and exercise to keep you in shape, both physically and mentally.

According to Gwen Rubinstein, senior editor of *Association Management*, men project status, power, and dominance, while women's body language says submission, affiliation, and passivity. Professional women and managers struggle to maintain their femininity while projecting a sense of power and authority. You can command that power; walk as if you share a proud thought.

Moving as you speak adds energy to your presentation as it helps get and keep the audience's attention. Besides, an audience can't hit a moving target. As you write your speech build in time for movement.

Four important times to move while making a speech are: (1) to make a point. When you need to stress a point, move closer to the audience; (2) to make a transition. As you make a transition from one point to another, walk from one side of the speaking area to the other, pause, then begin your next point. Repeat the process occasionally, but not too often. Walking back and forth across the stage too often appears as though you're pacing. And pacing is another sign of being nervous; (3) to get and hold the audience's attention. Let your movements convey a high energy level. The amount of energy and enthusiasm you display generates the same amount of excitement throughout the audience; and (4) when using a visual aid.

A few do's and don'ts for moving on stage:

• Don't send false signals. If you move inappropriately or inconsistently with your message, you send a signal that could be misinterpreted by your audience. Erma had the worst case of the wanders I ever saw. She couldn't stand still. She would walk out in front of the lectern, then quickly return behind it. She'd take a few steps to the right, then scurry back behind the lectern again. I asked her why she couldn't stand in one place. She said, "I thought I was supposed to walk around." She didn't realize until she saw herself on video how nervous and indecisive she looked.

• Never present a speech sitting down, even if you're talking to a small group. Standing gives you the advantage of a dominant position of authority, and allows your diaphragm more breathing room. Standing also gives you more freedom to move around. Moving also helps control nervousness.

• Don't close yourself off from the audience by folding your arms across your chest. I saw a woman do this as she introduced a speaker. Her introduction reeked of insecurity.

• Never move without a reason. Move to make better eye contact, to make a point, or to show visual aids.

• Don't slouch. It's important that you appear poised and confident. Stand on both feet. Slouching can be interpreted as lazy, tired, or give the impression you don't care. Relax, avoid appearing stiff and uncomfortable, even if you are. Walk tall, proudly, with a purpose. Project confidence and energy.

• Give yourself room to move. Suggest that a lectern be set up away from the head table. Speaking from behind a table limits your range of motion and ability to connect with the audience.

• Practice all your moves. Try stepping onto a platform in heels while wearing a straight skirt without wobbling or hiking your skirt. If you can't conquer the steps, reassess what you're wearing or practice walking up steps until you can.

BODY TALKING TIPS—A WOMAN'S VIEW

There once was a time when ladies of nobility and high breeding were exposed to poise and charm schools where they learned to walk, sit, and stand as ladies. Those days, for the majority, are gone, but the importance of the lessons remains: You must stand, walk, and sit with poise and control while commanding a sense of power and grace.

• The lectern lean. Men love to look casual under fire and lean on the lectern to appear relaxed and confident. For a woman, this gives the impression of trying to look like one of the big boys. For those women who stand under five feet tall, an elbow reaching to rest on the lectern can cause their clothing to hike up in a most unflattering manner. This doesn't mean that you must never lean on the lectern. Occasionally resting an elbow or hand on the edge of the lectern will give you a casual appearance. This can work for you or against you.

- Crossing the stage. Poise is the key. Taking small steps can make you look like a wind-up doll, while wide strides can make you look like you're walking behind a farmer's plow. Cross the stage with your shoulders facing the audience or continue facing the audience and cross one leg in front of the other. To turn, pivot on toe and heel. These movements may take a little practice, but they aren't hard to do.

- Walking among the audience. Audience contact is important for several reasons. First, it helps keep the audience's attention focused on you. Second, when showing a small object, moving among the audience allows them a better look, and finally, getting close sends a subliminal message that says, "I am confident, relaxed, and comfortable being with you."

- Find a mentor who has all the qualities of a good speaker and emulate her. Watch her gestures and facial expressions and learn from them. Adopt and adapt the techniques that you like and that feel comfortable to you. Also, watch and learn from speakers who you think aren't so good. Does she have any distracting gestures or annoying habits? Sometimes the best way to learn what to do is to learn what *not* to do.

6

From a Whisper to a Roar—
The Female Voice

That fine God-given instrument—the voice—must be
capable of responding with the greatest subtlety
to every shade of each emotion.

LOTTE LEHMANN, *More Than Singing*

The sound of your voice reflects your personality, attitude, and emotional state; and because your voice is a complex, living instrument, it must be properly developed, trained, and cared for. The more variety, vitality, and enthusiasm you can put into your voice, the more you'll hold your audience's attention. A dull, life-less monotone voice is a sure fire way to anesthetize your listener. Often women fear they lack a strong, powerful voice. But a strong and powerful voice is not always possible, nor is it desirable or necessary. Women can do many things to ensure vocal qualities that charm an audience while enhancing their message.

RX FOR A GREAT VOICE

Proper Breathing and Posture. Actors learn that breathing correctly is the key to a voice that carries to the back of a crowded theater. Without proper breathing and posture their voices will be flat and inaudible.

Standing straight allows room for the chest cavity to expand and fill the lungs with enough air to support your breath while speaking. Without enough air, you'll have to pause in the middle of a phrase or sentence to gulp air, making you look and sound nervous. I've watched many novice speakers breathe from their chest, their shoulders rising and falling with every breath.

To know if you are breathing correctly, stand in front of a mirror, relax, and breathe as you normally do. What part of your body moves? Is it your shoulders? Chest? Stomach? If your shoulders move, you're breathing from only a small portion of your lungs. Instead, force your abdomen to do the work by breathing from the diaphragm. Breathe without raising your shoulders or allowing your chest to move. Watch as the abdomen extends, filling with air. Now you're breathing correctly.

Michele Woods, radio personality and music director, suggests the following exercise for proper breath control: Place your fist in the pit of your stomach just below your rib cage, take in a deep breath. Feel the stomach muscles expand. Now, release tiny puffs of air as you say, "che ... che ... che...." You should feel the muscles jump, but remain firm. By practicing this technique, you'll strengthen your stomach muscles and produce a fuller sound. You can achieve the same results by closing your mouth and releasing tiny breaths of air through your nose.

Another technique is to lie on your back and place an object such as a book on your stomach. Breathe in and watch how the object rises, then lowers as you exhale. Practice these exercises until breathing from your diaphragm becomes a habit.

Projecting for Volume. Many women lack volume in their voice, making them appear weak and ineffectual, diminishing the power of their presentation. Perhaps they're self-conscious about speaking up. Maybe they're shy. It could be they swallow their words. Whatever the reason, the results are the same; if you can't be heard, you might as well not speak at all.

Female drill instructors who have soft voices can belt out commands as well as any male. The trick is learning how to project the voice from the diaphragm instead of from the throat.

Eben C. Henson, voice trainer, says in *How to Play the Voice as an Instrument* that projecting doesn't mean talking louder by shouting. Shouting only tightens the vocal cords, raising the pitch of the voice, and you don't want that. He says in order to project and have a fuller, richer tone, you must create deeper chest vibrations. To do this, place your hand on your chest and feel where the sound and vibrations come from as you say the words "*Me, My, Mo, Moo.*" Make your voice descend from the nasal cavity to the chest with each word. The *Me* sound comes from the nose, the *My* comes from the mouth, the *Mo* comes from the throat, and the *Moo* comes from the chest. Become accustomed to how that *Moo* sound feels. That's where you get the fullest and richest sound and the most volume.

How can you tell how much volume you need? The size of the room and the number of people in your audience are two determining factors that must be considered. Check your volume level before your audience arrives. If you have the opportunity to visit the room in which you'll be speaking, test your volume by asking someone to stand in the back of the room and listen to you as you talk in your normal speaking voice. Does your voice carry well? If they can barely hear you with the room empty, you won't be heard with the room full. As a solution, you can do one of two things: speak with more volume or use a microphone. (We'll talk about microphones in just a minute.) Asking if everyone can hear you is a sign of inexperience. What would you do if everyone in the back row raised their hands? Are you prepared to shout the entire duration of your speech?

Vary your volume to avoid "the monotonies." Train your voice to increase and decrease volume for variety and to hold the audience's attention. Work on increasing and decreasing your volume without straining your vocal cords as you repeat the following sentences:

I am speaking softly.

I am speaking loudly.

I am increasing my volume.

I am decreasing my volume.

As with all things in making a speech, learning to vary your volume will take practice—lots of it.

Rate of Speech. Just as you should vary your volume, vary your pace when you want to emphasize a particular point or when dramatizing a story.

The normal speaking rate is 125 to 150 words per minute. This doesn't mean you can't speak faster or slower than the norm. You want to speak fast enough to avoid putting the audience to sleep, but not so fast that you run words together, drop endings, or increase the pitch of the voice; and you need to speak slowly enough to be understood. But ultimately, you must vary the rate to avoid a constant pace that creates a dull and boring speech.

Speaking fast and breathlessly signals inexperience and nervousness. Early in my career, I was asked to speak to a group of senior citizens. The time allotted was twenty-five to thirty minutes. I selected a topic and set out to write and rehearse the speech. On the third run-through, a family member timed me. I was surprised to discover I had spoken for only ten minutes. I was sure I had at least twenty minutes' worth of material. That family member—my mother—in her ever-so-patient manner said, "Who's nipping at your heels? You ran through that speech like a wild dog was chasing you." I slowed down, thought about what I was saying, and put more emphasis where needed. Sure enough, I had my thirty-minute speech.

Different types of speeches require different pacing. Motivational speeches are usually faster paced, while informational speeches are slower, allowing the audience to absorb the information.

Your rate should be a natural extension of your personality. If you have a bubbly personality, you will most likely speak faster than someone who is more reserved. Remember your audience as you speak and adjust your rate of speech to their ears. If you were born and raised in the North and are speaking to southerners, slow down and match their listening rate. The reverse is also true. A northerner hearing a southerner will be silently yelling, "Get on with it. Say what you're going to say already."

Pitch.   One woman in particular caught my attention at one of my seminars. She was well dressed with tasteful and flattering jewelry, makeup, and hair style. Her image screamed "successful woman" who commands authority, but when she introduced herself, I was surprised to hear she had a shrill, high-pitched voice that sounded like a barn door with rusted hinges.

A high-pitched voice must be trained into a pleasant and authoritative voice. According to Carla Spencer, speech training pathologist, men's vocal cords are longer, thicker, and vibrate at a slower frequency, causing a lower pitch. A voice with a lower pitch creates the image of confidence and power. Because the woman's vocal cords are shorter, the opposite is true, giving women a higher pitch and a weaker sound. But, Spencer says, with proper training a woman can learn to maintain a pleasant and somewhat lower pitch.

There are times, however, when a higher pitch is useful; for example, when conveying excitement. Try saying, "I want that apple" with a high pitch. Then repeat the sentence with a lower pitch. The high pitch makes you sound like a spoiled child. The lower pitch sounds richer and more authoritative.

Did you notice that as you spoke with a lower pitch, you also spoke slower? There is a direct relationship to pitch and pace. The faster you talk, the higher the pitch. Slow down and decrease your pitch to a more pleasant sound. Another way to prove this point is to tape record your voice as you say the following nursery rhyme. First, say the rhyme slowly; then repeat it as fast as you can.

Hickory, dickory dock.
The mouse ran up the clock;
The clock struck One.
The mouse ran down.
Hickory, dickory dock.

Did you notice that as you spoke faster your pitch raised? Practice using the full range of your voice to increase its flexibility.

Inflection. By emphasizing a particular word, you give it more weight than the other words around it. Putting more stress on one particular word not only pulls the audience's attention to that word, it causes your voice to come alive with energy. It can also change the meaning of the sentence. Listen as you say the following sentence each time emphasizing the word italicized.

"*She* sat on that bench." By emphasizing the first word, *she*, we are told that no one else sat on the bench but the woman.

"She *sat* on that bench." With *sat* emphasized, we know that she didn't lie down on the bench, nor did she stand on it. She *sat* on it.

"She sat *on* that bench." Here we learn she didn't sit under, over, or near the bench but *on* it.

"She sat on *that* bench." With all the other benches in the park, she chose *that* particular bench to sit on.

"She sat on that *bench*." There were chairs and sofas to sit on, but she chose the *bench*.

Rhythm. In his voice classes, Eben Henson says that words have their own rhythm. They sound like the whole notes, half notes, and quarter notes of music. He says when you say the word *sea*, your voice creates a sound of an endless ocean stretching beyond the horizon. Say the word *buzz* slowly and listen to its sound. Hear its vibration and rhythm? What comes to mind when you hear the word *dawn?* You see the sun slowly rising, bringing with it a soft, rosy glow. Repeat "dawn." Stretch the sound and let your voice reflect that image.

Listen to the sharp staccato sound of the words *pop, tap,* and *kick* and the dragging whole note of the word *wind*. Slowly say the word *fall* and listen to how your voice trails downward.

Speak slowly and let your voice rise and fall, giving full value to each word you say. In other words, bring your speech alive by singing it. (In a manner of speaking.)

Cadence. When I hear the word *cadence*, I'm quickly reminded of a drill sergeant shouting "left, right, left, hup, twop, threep." She sets up a rhythm that makes marching more tolerable. That sing-song cadence is fine for marching but deadly for speakers. Some speakers have a set rhythm to every sentence. The most common is ending every sentence upward, making the sentence sound like a question.

Clarity. Don't be a mush mouth. Few things make listening more difficult than words smothered in mumbles or a raspy or gravely voice. Tape your speech and listen carefully to how clear you sound. Ask a friend to listen to your message. Did they have to strain to understand what you said? If so, you need to work on creating clearer understandable sounds.

Articulation. The days of elocution lessons are gone, leaving behind an "ing" deficit generation. The dropping of *ing* turns such words as *going* into *gonna* and *cooking* becomes *cookin'*. Lazy speech transforms "got to" into "gotta," "just" into "jist," and "probably" into "probly." We can use sloppy speech when talking to friends and neighbors, but at the lectern it's deadly.

I missed a speaker's point when I understood him to say "the fence." By the time I realized he had said "defense," he had shifted gears and was talking about something else.

Try this lip and mouth warm-up exercise. Place a pencil between your teeth and speak with your lips curled around the pencil. Form each word slowly, saying each syllable separately. Push the words around the pencil so they aren't hiding behind your teeth. After speaking like this for several minutes, remove the pencil. You'll find your mouth and lips move as if the pencil were still in place. Your words are clearer and more articulate.

Make a concentrated effort to enunciate precisely so that it forces you to speak more slowly and distinctly. Pronounce each syllable as though you were wrapping your tongue and lips around every word, tasting each one.

DELIVERY TECHNIQUES THAT ADD PIZZAZZ

The Whisper. There's a special power in the whisper. Watch two people sitting with their heads together, mouthing words. Ever wonder what secrets they are sharing?

Whispering creates mystery, causing the audience to lean forward, cock their heads to hang on to your every word, waiting for a great secret to be revealed. The whisper says, "This is especially important information. Listen up."

How can you whisper and still be heard? When I say whisper, I mean speak in a stage whisper. It's a little tricky, but with practice you can do it. Continue speaking with a lung full of air, project from the diaphragm, yet make the words sound as if they are whispered. A microphone makes this technique even easier.

The Dramatic Pause. Mark Twain said, "The right word may be effective, but no word was ever as effective as a rightly timed pause."

Timing is everything to actors and comedians. They use timed pauses in their delivery much as a musician uses a rest in a musical score. Many novice speakers worry about pausing too long between sentences, phrases, or words because they think that pausing makes them look as if they forgot what they were saying. But the opposite is true. Pauses used effectively add dramatic tension and cause the audience to listen more intently, wondering what's coming next. Pauses also help control nervousness by allowing you time to breathe. Think of pauses as commas and periods, punctuating your speech.

When is the best time to use a pause? Thomas Montalbo, speaker and author of the *Toastmaster* article "Say It With a Pause," says to use a pause after asking a rhetorical question. Give the audience time to absorb your message.

Pause after being introduced. Don't start talking the instant you reach the lectern. Pausing slightly when you first get to the lectern gives the audience time to settle down and center their attention on you. It also shows that you are poised and in control.

Pause to emphasize a particular point or idea. Montalbo suggests when saying something especially significant, challenging, or shocking, pause both before and after the statement. By pausing before, you send a signal that something important is coming. Pausing afterward gives the listener time to ponder your words.

Pause as a transitional device. A moment of silence when moving from one idea to another signals a shift of gears and gives the audience time to shift gears with you.

Pause as a signal that you're coming to the conclusion. A pause, along with transitional words and movements, lets the audience know the end is near. The pause adds drama to the end of an inspirational speech.

Always pause after a humorous comment, joke, or story. Give the audience time to laugh and giggle. Talking over the laugher irritates listeners when they can't hear what you say next.

And finally, pause at the end of your speech to let the audience know it's time to applaud. Milk the moment.

Put a Smile in Your Voice. Michele Woods says it's impossible to sound dull while you're smiling: "I'm always smiling when I'm on the air. Smiling makes my voice sound alive, enthusiastic, and friendly." When she trains other women radio announcers, she suggests they practice smiling while reading out loud. This technique will work for you, too. Next time you read a bedtime story to a child, put happiness in your voice by smiling.

Talk in a Conversational Tone. The best approach to any speech is to talk as if you are having a discussion with a friend over a cup of coffee at your kitchen table. (Without the dropped endings, however.) You are relaxed and comfortable. Because you know your subject, you speak with conviction. You automatically raise and lower the pitch of your voice, increase and decrease the volume, and change your pace. You use contractions and short words and sentences. Your voice is animated and alive with enthusiasm. It has energy, making it sound exciting. If you can talk that way to a friend, you can speak that way when making a speech.

Be Yourself. Have you ever watched a speaker who, as soon as he reached the speaking area, went into an act as if performing on stage? That's just what it is—an act—and it seldom fools anyone.

When making a speech, don't put on a different personality or become plastic. Don't lecture or preach. Your voice should be as natural as your gestures. The more natural you sound, the more believable you'll come across. The audience will see a real person, not a phony.

Develop a style that is comfortable for you. Are you generally enthusiastic and bubbly, or is your style more low-key? There is nothing wrong with either one. The important thing is to use *your* own style.

CARING FOR YOUR VOICE

Don't abuse your voice. If you overuse your voice, someday it will quit on you. Constantly straining your voice causes soreness or hoarseness; combine that with dry-mouth from nervousness and you have a big problem.

At the first sign of a sore, scratchy throat, stop talking and give your voice a rest. Dr. Raymond Olien, DMA, says should you become hoarse or get a sore throat, relax your vocal cords by sipping a combination of apple cider vinegar and honey mixed with hot water. He adds that gargling with a mild solution of warm salt water helps relieve dryness and soothes the throat, but it doesn't reach the vocal cords.

Don't clear your throat by repeatedly hacking; this only irritates the vocal cords. Try clearing your throat by pulling air through your nostrils and swallowing. The best thing you can do if your throat becomes dry or raspy is to *stop talking*.

Avoid three things: milk products, because they coat the throat, causing phlegm; throat lozenges, which numb the lining of the throat, giving a false sense of wellness; and whispering, which only aggravates the vocal cords more.

To eliminate the stressed-induced tightness in your throat and jaw muscles, follow these suggestions: Sit in a comfortable position and let your shoulders relax; rotate your head from side to side; stretch your neck left to right; front to back; let your jaw drop and say "ahhhhhhh" as you exhale; open your mouth in a wide yawn and let out your breath with a slight sigh. Do these exercises several times as needed.

Smoking also causes poor vocal quality. I'm not going to preach about the harmful effects of smoking, but medical reports reveal that years of smoking damage the vocal cords, causing a raspy or gravelly voice that grates on the ear.

VOCAL EXERCISES

It's time now for you to practice all the things you have learned in the last two chapters. Using the sentences listed below, stress one particular word within each sentence. Raise and lower your pitch and volume. Say the sentence fast, then slow. Turn the sentence into a question, then a strong statement; beg, sound angry, happy, and sad. Once you have mastered vocal variety, add hand gestures and facial expressions to match the words. Get the picture? Try this in front of a mirror, too, and have fun with it.

"Not in my backyard."
"The sun sets slowly in the west."
"You must be kidding."
"Come on up and see me sometime."
"Stop that."
"Strike three, you're out."
"But, I'm innocent."
"I'm so tired."
"Green slime oozed all over."
"Now, wait a minute."
"What did you say?"
"Shame on you."
"And now, here's Johnny."
See how many ways you can say "Ah," "ha," and "oh."

ROMANCING THE MICROPHONE

Women seldom have deep, bottom-of-the-well voices that vibrate off the walls; we need help in amplifying our voices. Whether you are a novice or a more experienced speaker, you should always consider using one vital tool—the microphone—to turn a faint, soft voice into a dynamic force.

Professional speakers, entertainers, and performers know the value of a good sound system. They use microphones to enhance the quality and volume of their voice. Plan to use a microphone when speaking to a large audience, to override the competition of rattling dishes, loud music, people talking, or emergency vehicles racing up and down the street outside, and, of course, for longer speeches that tire the vocal cords. Use a microphone to avoid straining your vocal cords while sustaining a good volume level.

If you have never spoken into a microphone before, the experience can feel strange and you need to become familiar with it before making a speech. Get to know the feel of the microphone and how your voice sounds as it reverberates.

There are several microphones on the market today, each with different capabilities. We'll look at two basic types, the microphone with a cord and the wireless.

The microphone with a cord is the most common, but if attached to the lectern, becomes a nightmare. It restricts movement, limiting your ability to use visual aids or to walk among the audience. You must stand in one place, facing the microphone, for it to work effectively.

The wireless handheld microphone is better and acts like a miniature radio station with a transmitter and receiver built into the handle. It has grown in popularity over the past few years because it allows you to walk about without the constraints of a cord. It has a crisp, clear sound and is reliable. It can also be placed in the microphone stand when not in use.

The wireless lavaliere microphone is small and can be looped around your neck or easily clipped onto your clothing. Its size and its ability to free the user to walk around, use gestures, work with visual aids, or demonstrate a product, make it a great tool. Because of its size, it tends to disappear, especially when on camera, and because the lavaliere isn't being moved around like others types, the distance between the microphone and mouth, about six inches below the chin, is kept constant.

For best results, a microphone should be held or mounted about six to twelve inches from the speaker's mouth, pointing up at about a 45-degree angle. Holding it closer can cause an unflattering bass-heavy sound.

The transmitter of the wireless microphone is contained in a small pack and worn somewhere on the body. It's important for women to know if they will be using a lavaliere microphone so they can wear appropriate clothing, such as a suit where the transmitter can easily be attached to the waistband with the jacket hiding it.

There is a disadvantage, however. The lavaliere rarely sounds good if handheld or used away from the body. For best results, don't clip the lavaliere behind a scarf or under the lapel of your jacket. This reduces the pickup of high frequencies, which results in a flat, "muddy" sound. Attach the microphone to a small stickpin, chain, or piece of jewelry and keep it away from loose clothing that might rub against it.

When using a wireless microphone, stay within one hundred feet of the receiver so you don't lose the signal. When using a belt-pack type transmitter, be sure the antenna cable isn't coiled in your pocket, causing the transmission distance to be significantly reduced.

DO'S AND DON'TS FOR USING A MICROPHONE

How many times have you seen speakers walk to the lectern, tap on the microphone, and say, "Can you hear me out there?" Fumbling with the microphone is no way to begin a speech, and using it incorrectly tells the audience you haven't done your homework. Never assume the microphone works or that everyone in the audience can hear you. Here are a few suggestions for making sure the microphone is working properly *before* you begin:

• Find out what type of microphone is available and, if possible, test it for sound level, tone setting, and placement before the audience arrives. Listen to your voice as it comes back to you over the speakers.

• Tap on the microphone gently. Talk across it, saying, "Test one, two, three" or "This is my normal speaking voice." Never blow into the microphone; it's harmful to the diaphragm.

- Have someone stand in the rear of the room and tell you at what sound level he or she can best hear you. Remember, when the room is full, the noise level will increase and you'll need more volume.

- Check to see if the little button on the side of the microphone is turned on. The speaker ahead of you may have inadvertently turned it off.

- Make sure that all loudspeakers are turned on. Many meeting rooms are designed in separate sections, each having its own sound system and separate controls.

- Don't hold the microphone horizontally in front or too close to your mouth. Doing so causes certain letters such as *P*, *B*, *D*, *K*, and *T* to be overemphasized, making a popping sound that blasts the sound system. It's best to hold the microphone vertically a few inches below your chin and talk across its head.

- Don't hold the microphone too far away either. You'll lose volume.

- Hold the microphone at a constant distance from your mouth. And don't gesture with the microphone.

- If you get feedback—that high-pitched squeal—there are several things you can do to eliminate it: (1) step away from the microphone, (2) aim the microphone away from the loudspeaker, (3) have someone lower the volume, or (4) move the loudspeaker away from the microphone so the sound doesn't come back to the microphone. Don't put your hand over the microphone; that will only make the problem worse.

- Shut the microphone off before you lay it down to avoid the clanking sound from coming through the speakers.

- Avoid the death grip. Hold the microphone gently between your fingers, relaxing your hand.

- Leave the microphone in the holder. Adjust it for the correct position only at the beginning of your speech. Then leave it alone. Don't fiddle with the microphone or the cord. Don't take the microphone out of the holder and play with it. This not only annoys the audience by causing inconsistency in volume, it makes you look nervous.

- Remember to turn off the microphone, especially if it's wireless. I heard a story about a speaker who became ill while speaking (now, there's a happy thought). He gave the audience a problem to solve and left the stage, heading for the restroom. After vomiting and flushing the toilet, he washed his face and regained his composure only to discover he had left the microphone on. The audience heard everything.

Even with all your efforts to insure the sound system is working, Murphy and his laws lurk around the corner waiting for you to begin your speech. For insurance, arrange for an assistant to stand in the back of the room during your speech and signal to you if something goes haywire with the system or let you know if the microphone goes dead. If you get the prearranged signal, *stop!* Call for the back-up system, if necessary, but don't continue until the sound level is fixed.

Let the audience know you realize something is wrong with the sound system and you prefer they be able to hear you. Tell the audience there will be a slight delay and suggest they chat among themselves. Say something humorous to those sitting near the front and ask them to pass it on to those in the back. Most importantly, let the audience know you care about the quality of your presentation. Of course, this might not work in every situation. You have to make that decision.

7

Visual Aids—
I See What You're Saying

*Experience has no textbooks nor proxies. She demands
that her pupils answer the roll-call personally.*

MINNA ANTRIM, *Naked Truth and Veiled Allusions*

Visual aids put punch and power into your presentation. Just as cartoons use words like *ZAM, SWAT, POW, ZOOM* to illustrate the action of the characters, visual aids add dramatic effect to a speech. They also help focus audience attention, provide strong visual support, and help the audience understand and retain your message. Visual aids turn ordinary into extraordinary.

Planning, creating, and using visual aids is only one link in the chain that makes up a good speech. Research shows that speakers who use visual aids and use them properly are perceived as better prepared, more professional, more credible, and more interesting and persuasive.

Key questions you should consider before making your visual aids are: What major points do I want to express? How can I best illustrate those points and make them as informative as possible? Which visual aid will best express those ideas? Which visual aid will work best for my audience and the environment? Will my budget allow for that type of visual aid?

Visual aids should be used to:

• Clarify a difficult or complex subject. Seeing how something works reinforces understanding. It is easier for the audience to understand the intricate details of an engineer's schematic or an organizational chart when these aids are shown.

• Save time. It is much faster to show how to do something than it is to explain it.

• Gain and retain attention. A sense of mystery underlies visual aids. As a visual aid flashes on the screen or an object is shown, people can't help but look. Visual aids provide variety and change of pace, keeping the audience glued to your message as they continue to focus on your visuals.

• Make your message more memorable. The chances of your audience remembering your message become greater when you couple your verbal message with visual support. You can say that a teenager eats on an average of 35 hamburgers a month or a total of 420 a year, but showing a picture of a blue-jean-clad teen standing hip high in hamburgers gives a clearer understanding of the figures and will be remembered longer than words. According to a report from the University of Minnesota, when visual aids are added to a presentation, retention is increased by ten percent (*The Toastmaster*, February 1990).

• Stimulate audience involvement. Ideally, you want the audience to become actively involved in your message, not just sit there passively. As you show a visual aid, the audience changes their listening posture. They know something has changed. They're intrigued. They study the visual aid, becoming more involved in the presentation.

• Control nervousness. An additional benefit for using visual aids is that it gives you something to do with your hands, a physical activity.

• Eliminate misunderstanding. When you can show instead of tell, the audience has a better and clearer picture of what you want them to know.

FIFTEEN TYPES OF VISUAL AIDS

1. *Overhead transparencies* (also called flimsies, acetates, foils, vu-foils) are most commonly used for briefings because they are inexpensive and easy to use. Overheads convey information clearly and quickly while allowing you to face the audience as you continue talking.

2. *Flip charts* (both floor and table top models) are useful in many speaking situations, but are best for smaller audiences. They can be prepared ahead of time, with blank spaces to be filled in as you speak and ask questions.

3. *Opaque projectors* are still around, but have lost popularity.

4. *Chalkboards* can be used for gathering information during a presentation. They allow you to write information, thoughts, and ideas quickly in brainstorming sessions.

5. *Charts, graphs, posters, photographs, maps, illustrations* are best for small audiences and are used to show trends, relationships, directions, and comparisons.

6. *Physical objects.* The actual object is far more impressive than a picture, allowing the audience to see the object's true size and features at close hand.

7. *Animals* are an ideal way to get the audience's attention as you hold up a sad-eyed kitten or puppy needing a good home.

8. *Slides* (35 mm) in a two-by-two-inch mount are frequently used because of their ease of handling and low production cost.

9. *Video tapes* can add to your presentation, but only when used for showing short examples that help illustrate a point.

10. *Audio tapes.* Caution! Audio tapes should be used for the sound effect only, such as animal sounds, music, or specific noises. Never use an audio tape to demonstrate someone speaking unless you're trying to demonstrate their speech pattern or speech defects. And never use an audio tape unless you have a quality tape and sound system.

11. *Handouts* are convenient for supplementing your speech and serve as a resource for later use.

12. *Your own body*—hand gestures, facial expressions, and body movements—are also a visual aid, and cost nothing to produce.

13. *Self-contained desk-top viewers* have limited use and are best for small audiences of approximately five to seven people.

14. *Flannel, magnetic, and hook-and-loop boards* serve well for storytelling.

15. *Multi-image/multimedia presentations* are without a doubt the most sophisticated and costly type of visual aid. It is described as two or more projectors programmed to dissolve from one image to another as music and narration support the visual images. With its animated computerized graphics, colored multi-images, and stereo sound spreading across the staging area, a simple flip chart and overhead transparency appear dull and obsolete by comparison. In addition, a multimedia production requires expertise by professionals in the field of visual arts and special effects, who must know how to produce the visuals and also have knowledge of the equipment required for the production.

WHEN TO USE VISUAL AIDS

An often-asked question is, "How do I know if I need a visual aid, and when is the best time to use it?" Use a visual aid when you want to:

- emphasize a key point
- explain terms, processes, and procedures
- illustrate a point and bring an abstract idea into focus
- present statistical data, making numbers easier to understand
- make comparisons, showing similarities between two or more concepts
- show relationships and point out correlations
- show an object too small or large to be realistically shown
- explain or show new or complex concepts or material
- show a new technique or give a demonstration of a new product
- restate your key points

WHICH VISUAL AIDS TO USE

Which visual aid will work best for your speech? The visual aid you decide to use will depend on the following:

1. *The type of speech being made.* Not all speeches require or lend themselves to visual aids. Informational and persuasive speeches can be made stronger with visual support. While inspirational and motivational type of speeches would not need visual aids. Neither would dedications, eulogies, awards, and farewells.

2. *Size of the audience.* A larger audience requires larger visual aids. While you can show much smaller objects to an audience of ten or fewer, showing an eight-by-ten-inch photograph to an audience of one hundred will fail—as would showing an overhead slide enlarged to ten by ten feet overpower a small audience of five.

3. *Physical environment.* Can the room accommodate your visual aids and equipment? If the room is too small to project your slides, you may have to consider using another type of visual aid. Every room is unique, with different problems. Lights that cannot be adjusted, obstructions that hinder the audience's view, electrical outlets not conveniently located, seats that can't be moved, and the lack of space to set up a viewing screen are just a few of the physical restrictions that can prevent you from using your visual aids.

4. *Equipment availability.* You can't show overhead slides on equipment that isn't available. And if you don't have your own equipment you will have to ditch the slides.

5. *Time requirement to prepare.* If you don't have time to prepare a well-made visual aid, don't. Some visual aids require more time to design and produce than others. Do you have three weeks to prepare or only two days? Assess the amount of time it will take to produce the quality visual aids you want.

6. *Time limitation during the presentation.* A ten-minute speech leaves little time to show fifty slides. You may want to chose another method of reinforcement.

7. *Ease of handling.* If you can take a twenty-pound turkey out of a 350 degree oven, you can handle a large stack of framed overhead slides, a flip chart, and a slide projector with its five slide trays. Most visual aid equipment today is lightweight and easy to handle.

8. *Cost.* Your budget and resources may be limited, but the quality of your visual aids should convey the best you can do. There is no excuse to ever display a sloppily made visual aid simply because you couldn't afford better. Many print shops have the ability to make high-quality overheads and handouts at a low cost.

THIRTY RULES FOR MAKING AND USING VISUAL AIDS

Poorly planned and constructed visual aids harm your presentation. If your message is important enough to invest time preparing and writing the script, it's important enough to take time preparing and producing a quality visual aid.

Follow these rules:

1. *Make sure your visual aids are necessary and relate to the topic.* Use visual aids only if they add support to your message and make the meaning more clear. The visual aid should be consistent with your purpose, but not the total vehicle for your message. Ask yourself, "Does the visual aid add to my presentation or distract from it?" "Does it enhance my speech?" "Does the visual aid illustrate my ideas clearly and accurately or will it confuse the audience?" If you're unsure, test its impact on a practice audience. Ask them what they see. If they don't know, the visual aid needs work.

2. *Don't use too many visual aids.* Are you making a speech or presenting a slide show? Not everything you say needs visual support. Don't put your audience on sensory overload.

3. *Each visual aid should demonstrate a single idea.* For example, if you're discussing three ways to improve work relations, don't include ways to handle incoming calls on the same visual aid.

4. *Use key words or phrases to express an idea.* Keep your visual aid simple and easy to read. Avoid using complete sentences. For example, the following is too much for a single slide.

• Eating less food at each meal satisfies hunger as it helps reduce calorie intake.

- Select foods that are low in fat and cholesterol and high in fiber.
- Eat more times during the day, as opposed to three large meals three times a day.

A better example would be:

- Eat in moderation.
- Be selective.
- Eat more often.

5. *Use no more than five words per line and no more than five lines per visual aid.* If you are discussing a complicated document that requires more than the recommended five lines, divide the information onto several slides. Place a page number and the word *continued* at the top right corner, for example, "Page 2 cont'd."

6. *The type should be large, bold, and clear.* When using overhead transparencies, 35 mm slides, flip charts, posters, photographs, et cetera, be sure the image is large enough to be seen by people in the last row. To make sure your visual aid can be seen by everyone, set it up and walk to the back of the room. If you can't see or read it, neither will your audience.

7. *Round off numbers.* Make your numbers "reader friendly" so your audience can recognize the numerical value at a glance. Eliminate zeros and decimal points whenever possible. Simplify complex equations.

8. *Use no more than four colors per visual aid.* Colors add excitement to visual aids, but too many colors become a circus. See the section on The Power of Color on page 109 for more detail.

9. *Use one—no more than two—typefaces.* Avoid stylized, ornamental script. This is not the place to show off what your new computer can do. Typefaces such as 𝕰𝖆𝖙 𝖎𝖓 𝖒𝖔𝖉𝖊𝖗𝖆𝖙𝖎𝖔𝖓, 𝕭𝖊 𝕾𝖊𝖑𝖊𝖈𝖙𝖎𝖛𝖊, 𝕰𝖆𝖙 𝖒𝖔𝖗𝖊 𝖔𝖋𝖙𝖊𝖓 are difficult to read.

10. *Use upper- and lower-case letters.*

A SENTENCE WRITTEN AND PRODUCED ON AN OVERHEAD SLIDE MAY BE COMPLETE AND UNIFIED AND STILL BE INEFFECTIVE BECAUSE IT'S TOO LONG AND THE AUDIENCE

CAN'T READ IT, OR BECAUSE IT WAS WRITTEN IN ALL CAPI-
TAL LETTERS.

Use Both Upper and Lower Case for Quicker Reading and
Easier Understanding.

Did you notice how your eyes slowed to read the sentence
in all caps?

Note: When using only one or two words on a slide, it is
acceptable to use all upper case letters.

11. *Be consistent in format.* Use the same typeface on all
slides and overheads. Place headings, logos, and text in the
same place on each slide, and be consistent with letter size and
color. If you use a border on one slide, use it on all slides. Title
each transparency and page of a flip chart.

12. *Dress up your visual aids with humorous cartoons, artwork,
graphics, illustrations, pictures, or drawings.* Keep them simple, use
only one per visual aid, and avoid gender stereotypes in graphics.

13. *Make charts, graphs, and diagrams easy to decipher.* When
using a line drawing, use solid lines. Use no more than six sections on a pie chart, shade each section with a different color
or shading, and place the largest portion at the twelve o'clock
position. Keep all words on graphs and charts horizontal. Don't
cause your audience to stand on their head to read the clever
slant you put on your headlines and information.

14. *Emphasize key points with bullets and dingbats.* Bullets
and dingbats are devices preceding a word or sentence. They
can be arrows, happy faces, or snowflakes. Keep them consistent on all visual aids. Use them in place of numbers when only
two or three ideas are being expressed.

15. *Give visual aids a psychological punch.* Place good news
or positive information at the top of a chart or overhead and
bad news or negative information at the bottom. Also, make the
overall transparency horizontal.

16. *Proofread all copy.* If you can't see your own typos and
misspelled words, have someone else proofread them.

17. *Check the seating arrangement.* Will everyone be able to
see your flip chart, graphs, and slides? Survey the room before
your audience arrives. With the room empty, you may be able

to see the flip chart from the back of the room, but when the seats are filled, it could be blocked. There will be times when you have absolutely no control over how the seats are arranged. If you can't rearrange the seats, you have two choices: rearrange the position of your visual aid for the majority of the audience or eliminate the visual aids.

18. *Set up your visual aids before the meeting begins.* Setting up your visuals after the introduction makes you look disorganized. Preset the video tape. It's annoying to watch a presenter fumble with the VCR trying to find the starting point. Place all overhead slides next to the projector with the first one on the projector, ready to go. Insure that the slide projector is set to the first slide and that your flip chart is in place.

Equipment is often set up by the hotel staff and placed in the position where the last speaker used it or where it is most often used. If your flip chart, for example, is not where you want it, request that it be moved or move it yourself. Don't be afraid to speak up and ask for the things you need to make your presentation a success.

19. *Don't stand between your audience and the visual aid.* That advice should be common sense, but you would be surprised how many speakers have no idea where they are on the podium and are unaware they are blocking the view.

20. *Keep visual aids and props covered until you're ready to use them.* Having an object displayed on a table in front of the audience is distracting. Once the visual aid is shown, give your audience several seconds to study it before discussing it. When you're finished, cover it or remove it from sight unless you will refer to it again later.

21. *Check all electrical equipment.* The first rule in working with any electrical equipment is to make sure it's plugged in and working properly. Have backup equipment just in case. Make sure the projector bulb isn't burned out and a spare bulb is on hand. Tape down all electrical cords. You certainly don't want to trip over a loose cord in the middle of your speech.

22. *Speak with more volume than normal.* For some reason, we can't look at something, analyze it, and listen at the same

time. As the audience reads words on an overhead, the speaker's voice diminishes, and because some electrical equipment has noisy fans and motors, you'll have to increase your volume to speak above the noise.

23. *Never allow props to be handled by the audience while you're talking.* They'll be interested in the object and tune you out. Examining a product or looking at pictures or handouts divides attention.

24. *Handle a prop only when you're making a direct reference to it.* Fiddling with an object before you're ready to talk about it draws attention to it, distracts, and makes you appear nervous.

25. *Hold objects so everyone can see.* If you're showing a picture, chart, or book, don't wave it around. Hold it still so everyone can get a good look. Better yet, hold it close to your heart so that attention is drawn to the object and you at the same time. Also, remember to leave the visual aid on the screen long enough for the audience to copy the information. And never read every word of the visual aid as if the audience can't read it for themselves.

26. *Keep visuals neat and free from scratches, bent corners, tears, and dust.* Your visual aids reflect upon you as a speaker. Don't present tired, worn-out visual aids.

27. *Rehearse with the same visual aids and equipment you plan to use during your presentation.* Projectors vary greatly in design and features. Not knowing how to turn on and focus the projector loses points when credibility counts.

28. *Speaking of rehearsing, DO!* Put as much practice into using your visual aids as you would into practicing the words you say. Don't allow a perfectly good speech to be ruined by awkward handling of your visual aids.

29. *Don't prepare visual aids too soon.* Changes may have to be made as your speech develops.

30. *Be flexible.* If anything will go wrong, it will happen while using visual aids. Show Murphy you won't be intimidated. Be ready to adjust to any circumstance that arises and always have an alternate plan.

This list of thirty rules for preparing and using visual aids may seem lengthy, but I want to stress one more time, visual aids should not be taken lightly. Much thought must go into their preparation, and much practice should be done with them before you ever step up to the lectern.

FIFTEEN SUGGESTIONS FOR USING OVERHEAD PROJECTORS AND TRANSPARENCIES

1. *Position the overhead projector on a skirted table, preferably off-center, and, if possible, separate from where you're speaking.* This has several advantages. First, you can position the table for optimum viewing, and second, it allows you freedom to move around so you aren't glued to one spot.

2. *Have the viewing screen placed high enough to be seen by the entire audience, preferably five feet from the floor.* Many rooms have a screen mounted to the wall, in which case the screen cannot be moved. You'll have to adjust accordingly. But be sure the projector and screen aren't placed too close together so that the image is wider at the top than at the bottom of the screen.

3. *Have all transparencies numbered and in order, sitting next to the projector, before your presentation begins.* Prepare a place to put the transparencies after you have shown them.

4. *Set the first transparency on the projector before your presentation begins.* Have the projector adjusted and prefocused. (Hint: If you're speaking in the same spot as the previous speaker and nothing has been moved, you won't need to make adjustments in the equipment.)

5. *Turn on the projector only when ready to show a slide.* Cover the light source when finished. Never leave a glaring white image on the screen. Avoid turning the light on and off; it wears out the bulb quicker.

6. *If one transparency is to follow another immediately, slide the second one on as you remove the first.* Make sure the transparency is positioned fully on the base of the projector so that no light leaks from around the frame. Practice doing this until the motion becomes smooth and comfortable.

7. *If you have several lines of type on one transparency, cover the portion not being discussed with a sheet of paper.* Slide the paper down the list to reveal only the information you intend to show. Revealing the entire transparency at once causes the audience to read ahead of you.

8. *To increase interest, try using the build-on technique of overlays.* For example, if you have five items that you want to talk about, simply tape five individual transparencies together and flip one transparency over the other. This works well for adding onto a diagram or graph. Each successive transparency adds additional information, showing the relationship to the previous one.

9. *Overhead transparencies can be used framed or unframed.* Both ways have advantages and disadvantages. Framed transparencies in cardboard mounts allow you to number them for easier organization and to jot notes on the frame for quick reference. Frames, however, are bulky and take more space.

Unframed transparencies are easier to pack for traveling but have a tendency to stick together. Place a sheet of paper between each one, preferably the original copy of the transparency. If using unframed overhead transparencies, tab and number each one along the edge with masking tape.

10. *Don't talk while changing transparencies.* Use the time to take a breath.

11. *Don't turn your back toward the audience and read from the screen.* Remain facing the audience and refer to the information on the transparency instead. This will help you maintain volume and eye contact.

12. *Use a pointer or pencil when indicating an item on the transparency.* Avoid using your finger and never use a pointer to call attention to words on the screen. Half of the audience will see a shadow and not the word. Also avoid laserlight pointers if your hands shake. If you do choose to use one, use it only briefly. And practice using it. It's annoying to watch a speck of light jump across the screen in an attempt to find a word. For best results, lay a pencil on the slide pointing to the item you wish to talk about. Leave it there until you are ready to talk about the next item.

13. *When showing transparencies with holes punched along the side, tape over the holes.*

14. *Make sure no extraneous light shines on the viewing screen.*

15. *When shipping slides or transparencies, always make a duplicate set, in case the original set is lost during transportation.*

SEVEN TIPS FOR USING SLIDES

1. *Number and arrange all slides in the order they will be shown.* If using more than one tray, number the trays.

2. *Make sure that slides are not backward or upside down in the carousel.*

3. *If possible, have an assistant help with the lights.* Ask the person sitting closest to the light switch to turn the lights on and off for you when you give him or her a prearranged signal. This will show a well-orchestrated presentation.

4. *As with the overhead projector, have a spare bulb on hand.*

5. *Use a remote control, if available, so you can move about and face the audience.*

6. *Make sure the table on which the projector is sitting is steady.* You don't want a shaky image on the screen. And, more importantly, have the projector leveled before you begin so you don't have to adjust the position while showing a slide.

7. *As a special technique, use a reverse image for greater impact.* When using reverse type, clear letters on an opaque background, use only a few words. A large amount of type is difficult to read and the letters tend to glare and run together.

Things to watch for and avoid when using projected material:

- the ability to control the lights
- low ceilings
- chandeliers
- windows with no curtains or blinds
- posts and pillars in the middle of the room
- screens that can't be moved

A disadvantage of using slides is that the room must be darkened, restricting the audience's ability to take notes.

FIFTEEN TIPS FOR USING FLIP CHARTS

1. *Make the letters large enough to be read from the last row in the back of the room.* Rule of thumb: The ratio for readability is one-half inch for each ten feet of audience distance. In other words, you'll need to make each letter on the chart at least two inches tall in order to be seen at a forty-foot distance.

2. *All words must be printed neatly and clearly.* Keep horizontal lines straight. Use a straight edge and pencil to make lines or use ruled paper. Space letters evenly and leave plenty of space between each word. The charts should be clean of eraser marks.

3. *Keep information simple so it can be read quickly and easily.*

4. *Tab pages for easy access.* Use predesigned tabs or make your own by folding masking tape over the edge of the paper. Color code or number the tabs so you won't have to sort through the pages trying to find your place.

5. *Alternate colors.* Use black or blue ink for words and use red or green to underline or to stress important points.

6. *Prepare major information ahead of time and fill in the rest during the speech.* Don't waste the audience's time by drawing a diagram or complicated illustration that you could have done at home. You can, however, write as you speak when involving the audience in a decision-making or brain-storming process. But have the major heading on the page beforehand.

7. *To avoid wasting time, cut masking tape in advance and tape sheets to the wall to be used as reference throughout the speech.*

8. *Just as you would reveal one line at a time on an overhead slide, you can do the same thing on a flip chart by taping a blank sheet of paper over the portion not being discussed.* Use drafting tape instead of masking tape; it won't tear the paper.

9. *Leave the first page of the chart blank or put only the title of your speech on it.* Place a blank page between each page containing information so the audience isn't distracted by the words bleeding through. When finished, cover the information with another blank page.

10. *Again, don't stand in front of the flip chart or turn your back to the audience while writing or talking.* Stand aside and use a pointer to direct attention to the visual aid so you don't block the audience's view, or have someone flip the pages for you, but rehearse with them first for timing.

(That brings up the question of using a pointer. Whenever I see someone use a pointer I'm reminded of a military leader standing at parade rest, one hand behind his back, the other holding a pointer as he slaps the chart, indicating the target for attack. He looks formal and stiff. I suggest you use your hand if you must point. But why point at all? The audience should be able to read the few lines on the chart. If not, perhaps something is wrong with the visual aid.)

11. *To speed things along, have someone who is a good speller and has nice handwriting write information on the flip chart as you talk.*

12. *Have ample light on the flip chart.* Many times the chart is positioned off to one side in less light than the lectern.

13. *Always use fresh pens and markers.* Use watercolor markers; permanent inks bleed through to the other pages.

14. *For a special technique, use a plastic overlay to write on to save having to remake the page for every presentation.*

15. *Use a sturdy, but lightweight easel.* One with folding legs will be easier to handle.

THE POWER OF COLOR

Just as using the right words gives special meaning to your message, the use of color adds a powerful dimension to your presentation. Color greatly influences the audience's perception of what you say. Color excites, persuades, and increases attention as it adds greater impact, emphasis, and increases retention and sales.

Each color has significant meaning and holds hidden messages that cause emotional responses. We see red when angry. We can feel blue. We become green with envy.

Red is a fierce color. It stimulates our senses, causing us to react. More specifically, red screams for attention. Fire trucks and emergency vehicles, stop signs, and those rubberized cones along the roadway that caution construction ahead are red for a reason. (Okay, so the cones are more orange than red.) They alert us to something happening, something important. STOP! Pay attention!

Yellow is the color of the sun, and invites friendliness as it surrounds us in its warmth, giving us a feeling of warm fuzzies. Yellow is mellow.

Green means "go." Green represents security, the earth, and lush meadows. Lighter shades are refreshing while darker shades represent strength.

Blue is tranquil and reflects a quiet dignity. It cools and calms us, creating a restful mood. Cool tones slow emotions and places a distance between the audience and the message. Darker shades such as navy command respect.

Don't overlook gray with its quiet neutrality. This neutral color is versatile and blends well with other colors.

White, in our culture, represents purity and virtue.

Black is strong, and although common, depicts sophistication and authority.

Leonard Meuse writes in his book, *Succeeding at Business and Technical Presentation*, that it's best to use cool tones such as light blue for background and warm colors for foreground material when producing visual aids.

Dan Wilson of Bacome/Wilson Group, an advertising and marketing firm, says the yuppie generation, who lived through the turbulent psychedelic '60s and '70s, and who are now in their mid-forties respond to colors that are bright and brave. Older groups, sixty-five years and up, are more conservative and prefer darker, more subdued colors.

SUGGESTIONS FOR USING COLOR IN YOUR VISUAL AIDS

1. *Not too many colors, please.* Just as you don't want to overwhelm the audience with too many visual aids, you also don't want to bombard them with too many colors. Limit colors on your visual aids to only four, no more than five.

2. *Be consistent with colors.* Choose the tone that best expresses the feeling or mood of your message and stick with it. Keep all headings, borders, and text in the same hue.

3. *Use warm tones for positive information and cool colors when showing the disadvantage of a solution or when you want your audience to respond negatively.*

4. *Yellow is powerful when used in a reverse image on a slide, but becomes difficult to read when used on white.* Avoid using yellow on overheads with a clear background, and never use it for words on a flip chart; the words become invisible.

5. *For a special touch, use a progression technique.* Highlight new information and words in a different color. For example, when discussing the countries of Burma, Canada, Egypt, and Poland, make four different slides. On the first, when making a point about Burma, highlight Burma in orange—show all other countries in a receding or darker color. On the next slide when the word *Canada* is revealed, show Burma and the other countries in a dark color while Canada is in orange.

6. *Use a contrasting color for emphasis.*

TIPS FOR MAKING HANDOUTS

I'm often asked, what should I include in my handouts? How do I make them?

Include detailed information you don't have time to present orally. Include the main points of your message, statistics, schematics, detailed diagrams, long quotes, graphs, and charts. When selling a product or service, you may want to pass along promotional material that gives addresses and phone numbers. Include references to other sources, studies, and research. You don't need to include everything you say in the handout.

Most informational-type speeches can use additional support in the form of handouts, but they're never used for inspirational, entertaining, or after-dinner speeches.

Handouts represent you or your company, and like visual aids, should be produced as professionally as possible. That means a good-quality grade of paper reproduced on a good copy machine or, if cost permits, professionally printed. If the audience is expected to take notes using the handout, select a paper without a gloss.

Color ink is often costly. Don't feel you must use color to make an impression. A quality black ink on white paper is effective. If you want to jazz up a handout, use colored paper. But avoid iridescent colors. Stay with pastels, buff, off-white, gray, or tan. And don't forget to incorporate copyright-free graphics and cartoons into your handouts.

If you're using several pages, keep them consistent with the same typeface, borders and headings. Number each page for easy reference and staple them so they can be handled comfortably. And if you really want to get fancy, and can afford it, place them in a folder.

There are many formats you can use. One is to leave a wide margin on the right or left side of the page for note taking. Another is a "fill in the blank" method. Leave plenty of space between lines for additional notes. Another method is to use the key words or phrases emphasized in your overhead slides. Some speakers make handouts of their overheads.

8

Practice Makes Perfect

*Opportunities are usually disguised as hard work, so
most people don't recognize them.*

Ann Landers

Swink's Law of Physics: The results of a speech are in direct proportion to the effort put into the preparation and practice of that speech. In other words, work in; success out.

I said in the introduction that you would have to do a lot of work if you intend to become an effective speaker. Now comes the time to put everything you have learned into practice. And I do mean practice!

Not every woman needs the same amount of practice time. There are some who can present information soon after it is organized in their heads. They're a rare breed. For the rest of us, hours of practice is the only road to a polished performance.

There are many ways to work through the process of practicing a speech. This method works best for me. Feel free to adjust the steps to fit your style.

THE TEN-STEP PROCESS

Don't begin practicing until you have your research, notes, and outline complete. If you begin too early and need to reorganize information, change quotes, add a story, or omit something, making changes can add frustration and confuse a novice speaker.

1. *Start by thinking about what you want to say.* How do you want the speech to sound and come across? Take each section and think about the information in that part. Think about the opening and where you want to place the emphasis. How will you state your purpose?

Then think through the middle, the main points, and subpoints. And last, think about the ending. Go through this mental outline several times until you have the speech thoroughly fixed in your mind.

2. *Begin verbalizing the speech.* If you have written your speech word for word, read it through. How does it sound? Smooth? Does it have a rhythm? Practice putting your speech into chunks of information. Work on one section at a time. Go through the opening, often the most difficult part, until you begin to feel comfortable with it. Next, run through the body of the speech. Don't worry if you miss a point. Make notes of the point missed and keep going. Finally, verbalize the ending.

Verbalize the entire speech without a break. Pause. Take it slow. Don't worry about the timing. Read through the speech several times for continuity.

This is a good time to find out if you can see your notes without glasses. Will you need to wear them? If you wear bifocals, at what height will the lectern need to be in order for you to see your notes?

3. *Next, practice using vocal variety.* Go though the written text and find words you want to emphasize and underline them in red. Mark the script with (PAUSE) where you feel a pause would be effective. Use arrows to indicate places where you want to raise or lower your pitch and wavy lines to show where you wish to change pace.

4. *Now, you're ready to tape record your speech.* Yuck! I know, you don't like the sound of your voice. Forget it. Few women like the way they sound when they hear their voice played back on a tape recorder. Don't worry about it. You're the only one listening to the tape.

Listen for filler words such as *ah, um, uh,* and the *you knows* that creep in between the real words. You might be surprised how many *ah*'s there are. One or two might be acceptable for a novice speaker, but your goal should be zero.

Listen for clarity of the words. Did the phrasing sound awkward? Did you stumble or have trouble pronouncing any words? If so, change them to ones easier to pronounce. Are the sentences too long? Did you have to stop and take a breath during a sentence? If so, shorten it. How's your diction? Did you mumble or drop the ending of certain words? Did you speak so fast that words ran together? Too slow? Did you place the right amount of emphasis on the appropriate word for the meaning you want to convey? Was your volume level audible? Did you need more volume in only a few places or over all? Is your voice pitched too high? Are you using vocal variety?

Time your speech. Don't worry if you run short on time at this point. Many speakers rush to get the speech over before they forget what they wanted to say. The solution to being short on time, unless it's way too short, is to simply slow down, breathe, and pause more often. If your speech ran overtime, you may have to trim information.

5. *Now add gestures.* Make each gesture count. What word or phrase would be better understood if you used a gesture to demonstrate it?

6. *Add visual aids.* Go through the speech again using your visual aids. Practice until they become easy and natural to handle. Check the timing again. How did you do? Remember, timing is critical to a good speech.

7. *Next, wear the clothing you plan to wear the day of your speech.* While in front of the mirror, take special notice of how the outfit moves with you when you gesture. Does the jacket ride up or do the buttons pull in front? Does your slip show

when you raise your arms? Remember, you are a visual aid, too. Don't allow your clothes to become a distraction.

8. *Make a video tape of your speech.* Set up the camera to show your entire image. Go through the speech again. As you watch the video, pay special attention to your gestures and body movements. Watch your posture. How are you standing? Is your weight on both feet? Are you standing in one place too long?

Say phrases of your speech—not the entire thing—and watch your hands. Do your gestures look natural? Are your hands talking too much? Look for those awkward or repetitive gestures. Watch your facial expressions as you say particular phrases. Do your expressions match the meaning of what you want to say? Can you make them more meaningful? Are you smiling?

This is a second opportunity to listen to how you sound. Listen carefully to the overall quality of your voice.

Are your notes visible? How do you look while using visual aids? Awkward? Smooth? Are you blocking them from view? Scrutinize your clothes.

Using all the tips and suggestions from the previous chapters, go through your speech several times and check to see if you can improve upon any of these areas. You probably can.

Wait! You aren't through yet.

9. *Practice visualizing your audience watching you.* When I practice, I always picture an audience. It helps me to feel the feedback, the electricity that comes from them.

Now, I'm going to tell you something that nobody knows and if you tell anyone I'll deny it. I line up all my stuffed animals—my real dog, too, if she's not off chasing leaves in the yard—and pretend they're my audience and I practice my speech for them.

10. *Finally, audience-test your speech.* Rehearse in front of family members or friends. Direct them to listen and watch for specific things like organization and logical flow. Ask them to listen for annoying speech habits and watch for distracting gestures. Ask one person to listen carefully for filler words and count them. You may be surprised at what you learn. Let them know you need their honest feedback, not a whitewash of praise.

If you have done all of the above, you will have rehearsed your speech a minimum of ten times.

There is a right and wrong way to approach practicing. Practice an hour every night for five nights. Don't cram five hours of practice into the night before the speech. The more time you have to absorb the material the better.

Can you overpractice? I say, no, you can't. You will know when you feel comfortable with your ability to give the speech without forgetting what you want to say. However, you want to stop when you begin to sound robotic.

ONE FINAL STEP

With all the preparation and rehearsal behind you, you still can do a few things to insure a smooth-running presentation.

First, do something special for yourself. Get your mind off the speech. Relax with a good book, walk through the mall, enjoy a double dip of chocolate ice cream, oh heck, make it a triple.

Second, get a good, full night's sleep. We have so much on our minds already with work, kids, and family, and making a speech only adds to the stress, making falling asleep difficult. It's easy to tell someone else to relax when you're not the one giving a speech, but you can try the following suggestions:

Soak in a nice warm bubble bath. Relax and *don't* think about the speech. Free your mind of all thoughts. One woman in my seminar told me she practices yoga. Another drinks a glass of warm milk.

If you're speaking early in the morning, lay out your clothes the night before. Have everything ready to go. Murphy shows no mercy for late risers who run around frantically in the morning looking for a lost belt or earring.

Charlene Bunas, a financial advisor in Santa Rosa, California, tells the story about how she dressed in a hurry only to find after her speech that a pair of pantyhose she had tucked away in the leg of her jumpsuit and forgotten had slowly slid down her pant leg and trailed along behind her during her speech.

I've heard other stories of speakers who presented in slippers, mismatched shoes, and skirts on backward. These women must have been in one big hurry to get to the lectern. The mind seems to go into hibernation the last few minutes before a speech. That's all the more reason to check every detail.

To avoid these problems, make a checklist. I set things like the overhead projector, extension cords, extra projection bulb, viewing screen (if necessary), handouts, pencils, markers, flip chart, et cetera, by the front door. The larger and heavier things I put into the trunk of my car the night before. I've snagged too many pair of nylons the day of a speech not to have learned that lesson. Make your checklist early during the preparation stage. Add to it as the need occurs. Have everything ready and check the list again before leaving the house.

EMERGENCY SURVIVAL KIT

Check each item. Make sure you have everything you may need for that emergency.

____ notes

____ your introduction

____ all visual aids, supplies (e.g., fresh markers), and equipment

____ sewing kit or needle and thread (same color as clothing)

____ cosmetics—lipstick, face powder, mirror, comb

____ facial tissue or cloth handkerchief

____ (when traveling): belt __ scarf __ jewelry __ shoes __

____ extra pair of nylons

____ feminine hygiene products

____ prescription medications and cough drops, aspirin, antacids, et cetera

____ tiny flashlight with fresh batteries

____ pencil and paper

____ masking tape (good for quick hem mending)

_____ duct tape for securing extension cords

_____ extension cord

_____ umbrella, rain bonnet, and rain boots

_____ map of location

_____ name and telephone number of contact person and meeting location

9

Platform Techniques and Etiquette

I was excited. I was confident, too. I don't mean that I wasn't nervous, because I was. But I was nervous and confident at the same time. Nervous about going out there in front of all those people, with so much at stake, and confident that I was going to go out there and win.

ALTHEA GIBSON, *I Always Wanted to Be Somebody*

A good speech can be made better by careful attention to details and knowing how to approach and leave the lectern, use notes, handle questions, and how and when to use handouts.

CONTROLLING LAST-MINUTE JITTERS

The last few minutes before making a speech can seem like waiting on death row for the warden to lead you away. Those butterflies fluttering in your stomach for the past several days have turned into kamikaze dive bombers. When this happens, you're ready. For me, it's an exhilarating experience that says, "YES, GO FOR IT!"

Now, it's your time at the lectern. The audience is waiting. Your heart suddenly starts to pound, knees turn to rubber, hands become clammy, and your mouth becomes dry as desert sand. You're sure your throat is swelling shut. You wish you could run and hide and never come out. Yep, that's the last minute jitters.

Stop that. You're going to do fine.

Before You Begin. Release the tension. In the few minutes just before making a speech, muscles begin to tense, adrenaline pumps, and you start to feel shaky. Recognizing the symptoms of nervousness is the first step in dealing with it. Begin by walking around. Stretch your legs and flex your knees. Allow your arms to dangle freely by your side. Stretch them high over your head, then reach for the floor. Shake them out, letting all that nervous tension flow away. Rotate your head from side to side in tiny circles; roll your shoulders in the same manner. Feel the muscles in your shoulders relax. Do a little wiggle. Doesn't that feel good? Learn to develop a relaxation method that works best for you, that feels good, and gives you a sense of well-being.

Warm up your vocal cords. Vocalize for two or three minutes just before you are introduced. Hide in the restroom or somewhere quiet and run up and down the musical scale by saying "la la la la la," "me me me me," "so so so so so," "goooooood." And believe that you are SO GOOD. Take deep breaths while relaxing your vocal cords. Mike Pruitt, the football player, said he did deep breathing and meditation exercises one to two hours before a game to help control his nervousness. Take in a deep breath then let it out slowly to the count of 1 . . . . . 2 . . . . . 3 . . . . . Do this several times and let the tension begin to melt away.

Visualize success. Pump yourself up for the presentation. Don't just think success, experience it. Stand quietly in another room, close your eyes, and visualize the room in which you'll be speaking. Get comfortable with those surroundings. Imagine the room slowly filling with smiling people. They're chatting among themselves. They're excited about hearing you speak.

You're being introduced now. Picture yourself walking to the lectern. Listen for the applause. Look out into the audience. Don't speak yet. Pause. Relax. Turn and face the smiling audience. Take a deep, cleansing breath. Now, begin your opening remarks. See yourself presenting the speech. The audience laughs at just the right moment; they're taking notes. They're asking questions and you have all the right answers. You make your closing remarks and hear the applause. No, not just applause, picture the audience giving you a standing ovation.

That wasn't so difficult, now, was it? Tell yourself again that you're prepared, you've done your very best, and now you're going to make a great presentation.

Judy Zinn, founder of Plaza Performance Group, a training and consultant firm, says she visualizes success. "I perform the way I visualize myself performing. If I visualize that I'm nervous, I will perform that way." Judy also says she owes a lot of her success to spiritual guidance. If saying a prayer to a higher power works for you, by all means, do it.

Maintain a positive attitude. Nothing is more self-defeating than negative self-talk. If you tell yourself you're going to do poorly, you will. It's that self-fulfilling prophecy again. Be positive about your ability. Wrap yourself in a blanket of confidence as you walk into the room.

Say to yourself, "This speech is going to go well. I know what I have to say. I'm going to get through this, and everyone will like my speech. I am prepared and ready to do a great job. This audience wants to hear what I have to say and they'll love me." Whisper to yourself you *are* somebody special. By making a speech, you aren't setting yourself up for failure; you're opening the doors for success. Seize the opportunity and bask in its glory.

One last but important thing to remember. Those last-minute jitters often cause a nervous stomach. It's a good idea to decide early if you should eat before you speak. I don't recommend a heavy meal. A light salad works, sometimes a piece of buttered bread, but you should eat something. Your body needs nourishment, especially when you are burning energy. I suggest eating an hour before a speech. If you have been invited to speak at a luncheon where a full meal is served, let your contact person know that you prefer either not to eat or have something light. Eating also wears off your lipstick. If introduced at the end of the meal without a break, you won't have time to go to the restroom to check for food stuck on your face or between your teeth.

Don't drink alcohol before you speak. You may think a drink settles your nerves—don't believe it. A drink can dull your enthusiasm, hinder your performance, and cause you to slur your words. Also avoid carbonated beverages; order tea instead. I forgot once and drank a soda just before a presentation. I burped my way through it. Not a pretty sight. Eating or drinking anything with caffeine can also be detrimental to your performance. Your nerves will be jangled enough without the help of caffeine.

I advise against taking tranquilizers. You want to remain sharp and alert. If you feel you absolutely can't get through a speech without taking a drug to calm you, you may need to reconsider making the speech altogether.

Just Before You're Introduced.   Be ready to walk on stage. Don't let the audience wait for you to stand, gather your notes, and find your way to the lectern. Stand close to the platform and begin walking as you hear your introducer announce your name. Don't sit in the back of the room where you need to maneuver around tables, chairs, and people's legs to get to the lectern. Don't sit with your legs crossed. A leg could fall asleep, causing you to limp your way to the lectern.

Watch your step. Beware of the audience member who might suddenly decide to stretch a leg—into the aisle—just as you approach. I hate to visualize that scene. Take a quick glance at the floor to make sure no electrical cords are in your way.

Tell yourself one last time that everything is going to be just fine; you are going to be great.

At the Lectern.   One speaker walked to the lectern, slammed her notes down on the lectern, leaned on it, and said, "Okay, here goes." Another speaker began his speech as he walked to the lectern. Those in the back of the room missed what he said before he reached the microphone. His opening remarks were spoiled.

Yet another speaker stood at the lectern, fumbled in his jacket pocket for his glasses, held them up to the light, and looked through them, put them on, took them off, wiped them with a handkerchief, put them back on again, took his notes out of his pocket, unfolded them, sifted through them, looked out at the audience (I guess to see if we were still there), cleared his throat, then began his speech. Give me a break! We sat there waiting and wondering when this man was going to start. Effective as an attention grabber? Perhaps. But it also diminished his effectiveness because he appeared unprepared.

By contrast, I saw a woman begin her speech by dramatically setting her bifocals on her nose. She glanced at her notes, then looked at the audience and said, "One of the many wonderful advantages of maturity." As we get older, we can get away with more—I have discovered.

I know of several professional male speakers who, when introduced, run up to the platform, ignoring the steps, and hurdle the riser in one easy bound. Can you imagine doing this while wearing a skirt? Although this approach to the lectern is exciting and full of energy, many people would look foolish attempting such a stunt. What can you do to project a high level of energy?

Approach the lectern, not at a run, but walking briskly and confidently. Remember to smile. Hold your head high, keep those shoulders back, and tummy tucked in. This is the first impression the audience has of you; make it count. Don't pull yourself to the lectern as if this is the last thing on earth you want to do. And for goodness sake, don't adjust your skirt, jacket, scarf, or hair!

Now, just as you visualized it, pause, look out at the audience, make sure they are ready to listen to you. It could be that they are shuffling papers, moving chairs, or the like. Take a deep breath and find a friendly face for reassurance.

Take your time—not as much as the gentleman did with the dirty eyeglasses, however. The pause may seem like an eternity, but it isn't.

Have your notes in hand. Don't go searching for them at the last minute.

Lay your watch on the lectern. Don't rely on a clock being on a wall, and even if it is, you don't want the audience to see you looking at it. Not only is this distracting, but appears as if you can't wait to finish and sit down. Make sure you have the watch in your hand before reaching the lectern instead of fumbling with the clasp, trying to take it off.

Speak loudly and clearly, with confidence and authority. Make those first words count.

Avoid locking your knees. Ever wonder why soldiers pass out during parade ceremonies? They locked their knees, cutting off circulation. When I was in the military, one of the first things we learned in basic training was how to flex our knees while standing at attention for long periods of time.

If you're nervous or if you have a stationary microphone, you can become riveted in one spot. Flexing your knees while wearing a skirt will never be noticed. Stand squarely on both feet and slightly bend one knee at a time without bobbing. If you're standing behind the lectern it's even easier. Flexing your knees takes practice, but then you have had lots of that by now.

Finally, concentrate on your message, not on the audience sitting there looking at you. Remember, you have something important to say and they want to hear it. By focusing attention away from your anxieties you allow yourself to stay focused on your message.

During the Delivery. Pace yourself. Start with a high energy level, then vary your energy during the presentation. Increase and decrease your energy level as you would increase and decrease volume. Maintaining a high energy level throughout your entire presentation will wear you out, make you look phony, and leave your audience dizzy as they attempt to keep up. Whether presenting an informal presentation on building a patio deck or motivating your audience to take charge of their lives, build to the end. Give those last remarks all the energy you have and leave the audience wowed by your performance.

Find courage to move from behind the lectern. Standing behind it blocks you from the audience and is too formal. Connect with your audience. Move closer as you relate an intimate story.

DISTRACTING HABITS TO AVOID

Agatha Christie wrote in *Witness for the Prosecution,* "Curious things, habits. People themselves never knew they had them." How true. We seldom realize we have gestures that reveal much about who we are. For example, a nervous laugh signals lack of confidence. Gestures toward the face are a sign of insecurity. I know a woman who slaps the side of her leg at the end of every statement as if for reassurance that what she said was correct.

Some of the more common and distracting habits women have at the lectern are:

• Swaying back and forth. Don't become a pendulum. The same goes for pacing. If you have reason to move across the platform, do so, otherwise plant your feet and move only when necessary.

• Repeatedly using a mannerism. Some speakers don't know what to do with their hands. As a result, they find a comfortable gesture and use it repeatedly for every point they make. As I said earlier, all gestures must have a purpose, and not everything requires a gesture.

When not using your hands, simply keep them at your side. Don't stuff them into your pocket. It makes you appear casual in a formal situation, or indifferent toward the audience or subject. It's okay to put your hand in a pocket occasionally, but don't do it as a crutch, or to hide your shaking hands.

• Frequently clearing your throat. Don't clear your throat out of habit; it's annoying and is a sign of nervousness. Radio personality Michele Woods suggests a spoonful of honey to soothe the vocal cords. Lemon also works well to clear away phlegm and mucus.

• Adjusting glasses. This is a common problem for every wearer of glasses. The frames loosen and slide down the nose. If your glasses are loose, have them tightened and adjusted.

• Fiddling. If you want to shout "I'm nervous," just fiddle with your props, pencils, jewelry, a strand of hair, visual aid equipment, microphone, or microphone cord.

- Shuffling your notes. Constantly shuffling through your notes looking for your place makes you appear nervous and disorganized. If you use notes, put them on the lectern and then leave them alone. Slide the top note card to one side when finished with it.

- Repeatedly saying filler words: *ah*, *um*, *you know*, and *so*. I firmly believe the first two words in the English language are, *Well, ah*. Watch any TV news program or game show when the reporter or host asks a question; you'll notice the person responding will begin by saying, *Well, ah*. And the *ah*'s don't stop there; they are peppered throughout our speech unknowingly. Filler words are distracting, annoying, and unprofessional. The best way to find out if you're guilty of repeatedly using filler words during your speech is to listen to the recording you made earlier.

Just what is too many filler words? When a filler word becomes noticeable, it's too many. It is not uncommon for even the best speakers to slip in an *ah* once in a while, but you'll never hear them repeat *well*, *ah* and *you know* so often that it becomes annoying.

- Gripping the sides of the lectern. The lectern is for holding notes and supporting the microphone, not you. I've seen women hold on to the lectern until their knuckles turned white. When you know your topic, you should feel comfortable enough to walk away from the lectern, at least long enough to make contact with the audience.

- Tugging or readjusting your clothing. I once saw a woman step up to the lectern, tug on her girdle with both hands, pulling it up under her belt, and then adjust her bra strap, seemingly unaware of her actions. I didn't make this up. It actually happened. I point it out because what a woman does in the first few seconds of taking the stage can make or break her performance and credibility.

If your dress, skirt, or jacket doesn't fit well, or if your undergarments are too tight or loose, make the necessary adjustments before you begin to speak. Don't be like the girdle tugger. Once you get to the lectern it's too late to make adjustments. By rehearsing in the same clothing, you'll have noticed any problems. Sometimes tugging at your clothes is just a nervous habit.

• Awkward body posture. Standing on one foot has the tendency to cause the opposite hip to stick out. I don't know about you, but I don't need help making my hips look bigger. Avoid putting your hands on your hips or holding one shoulder higher than the other. Stand straight with both feet flat on the floor. Don't point the toe of your shoe toward the ceiling or stand with one foot behind you, pointing the toe toward the floor.

• Annoying speech patterns. Avoid ending every sentence with the ending trailing upward or using a sing-song rhythm as in a recitation.

• Rolling your eyes. Constantly looking upward or to one side as if looking for divine guidance appears as if you have to think about everything you say.

TIPS FOR HANDLING NOTES

I make no secret that I use notes during my seminars and workshops. I can't remember all thirty rules for using visual aids; the list is too long, and I won't trust that amount of information to memory. The notes help me stay on track even though I know what I want to say about each rule.

There's no need to hide notes, but don't let them become a distraction. When writing your speech, use one side of the paper, write in large print, and as an extra technique, make a tiny fold in the lower left or right corner of the paper to make moving the page easier. This also prevents pages from sticking together. When finished, slide the note card or paper to the side. Don't flip it over, especially if you're using sheets of paper.

Use the same notes when delivering your speech as you did when practicing. Become familiar with where the words are on the paper or card so that only a quick glance will help you find your place.

Do not place your notes on the lectern ahead of time. Someone speaking before you may accidentally pick them up. Avoid talking while looking down at your notes. You'll lose volume. Refer to the notes only for what comes next.

To insure that your notes stay in order, place them in a ring binder when speaking outdoors. A gust of wind, and your speech is over. Wouldn't turning the pages be a distraction? Yes, but it's the lesser of two evils—seeing pages turn or float away on the breeze.

A question I am frequently asked is, "Do I take my notes with me when I step out from behind the lectern to cross the stage?" I suggest that because you have practiced this speech so much and because you know your material so well, you can leave the lectern for the few seconds it takes to make contact with the audience. Begin moving at a point where you can leave your notes without worrying that you'll forget something. Walking away from the lectern while continuing to talk makes you appear relaxed and confident. If you don't feel comfortable without notes, make them small, cup them in the palm of your hand, and carry them with you.

One last word about notes. Keep them neat. Scribbled ink-stained notes, if seen by the audience, can be a distraction.

READING VERSUS MEMORIZING
VERSUS EXTEMPORANEOUS

"Should I try to memorize my speech?" Memorizing a speech has a powerful effect but it also has drawbacks. I say memorize if you are in a speech competition, otherwise know your subject so well you can sit down with me over coffee and tell me everything you're going to say.

Memorization is dangerous. Even if you're familiar with your subject, memory lapses can happen. Plus, a memorized speech can sound robotic.

There are other opinions, however. John R. Powers, author and professional speaker, says by all means memorize. "You don't use notes to talk to your friends or neighbors. Why would you need notes to talk about something you feel strongly about?" he said.

Powers practices a method used for memorizing called "Topology," meaning location. He memorizes by mentally picturing a baseball field and placing each part of his speech in a particular section of the stadium. As he pictures the stadium in his mind, he recalls what part of his speech is there and then talks about it.

But Powers is a professional speaker with years of experience. Should you try to memorize your speech? Unless you are an experienced speaker, my advice is no. It's too chancy for a beginner; even more experienced speakers can forget what they wanted to say.

There is one exception, however. You can memorize the first couple of sentences of your speech or the conclusion, especially if you use a quote. Memorizing the opening of the speech allows you the freedom to look out at your audience and connect with them right from the beginning. And memorizing a quote as a conclusion for an inspirational speech, using dramatic pauses and gestures, makes your speech more emotional. I've seen this done and usually go away with tears in my eyes. Reading the quote would lose that powerful effect. In contrast, reading a quote insures its exactness if the quote is lengthy.

Another question often asked is, should I read my speech? Public relations personnel who must state company policy accurately, scientists presenting technical or scientific papers, and government officials who must be precise in their language read from a prepared manuscript.

On September 13, 1993, at the signing of the treaty between Israel and the Palestine Liberation Organization, speeches were read to insure accuracy. These speeches will be reprinted and referred to and quoted by historians. It would not do for the speaker to say one thing when something else is in writing.

The danger of reading from a manuscript, if not done well, is that you can sound too formal, lacking warmth and sincerity. The speech will be dull and lifeless, as if you're a machine repeating preprogrammed words and ideas. And, most importantly, reading causes poor eye contact. If you lose your place, you may have difficulty finding it again, and how can you expect to handle spontaneous remarks or questions when reading from a prepared script?

If you must read a manuscript, practice reading it until you become thoroughly familiar with its contents, improving your timing, enunciation, and vocal variety. Print the speech with only a few words or phrases on each line. You should be able to say the line in one breath. Set your pace for pauses, allowing time to look at the audience, gesture, and smile.

It is common today to see people read speeches. First, because of the pressure placed on them to perform perfectly, and second, because they lack time to prepare. One woman said she is often given little notice for presenting a speech. All the more reason for you to begin now learning the basics so you can circumvent the pressures of making a successful presentation on the spur of the moment. Once learned, those techniques are not forgotten.

Reading the speech provides more security for those lacking confidence. Both sides—reading and memorizing—have good arguments. Whichever you choose will depend on the situation, your personal preference, and experience.

Ultimately, the best way to deliver a speech is extemporaneously. Extemporaneous is not the same as impromptu. Impromptu means to speak without preparation. An extemporaneous speech has been researched, developed, and written with an expressed purpose in mind. It's planned and rehearsed. But it doesn't appear that way when delivered. An extemporary speech is delivered in an easy, natural manner, without reading a script.

Speaking extemporaneously allows greater eye contact and interaction with your audience. You'll appear more relaxed, handle visual aids, and field questions more easily because you aren't tied to a memorized script. The best approach to any speech is to speak from the heart, not memorize by heart.

QUESTIONS, QUESTIONS, QUESTIONS

There will always be questions when you are attempting to persuade or inform, especially if your topic is controversial. The question and answer session of any presentation is an opportunity to expand, clarify, and reinforce your message. Answering questions gives you feedback from the audience and gives the audience an opportunity to be part of the communication process.

Questions from the audience at any time during your speech can throw you off track or cause you to run overtime. Set the rules and guidelines during your opening remarks by instructing the audience as to when to ask questions—anytime during your speech, at specific times, or after you have finished. The important thing is to let the audience know what you expect of them.

Responding to Questions. Never prepare a speech without considering questions your audience may ask. If you've done your homework, you'll know the demographics of the audience and how much they already know about the subject. Anticipate what, if any, objections or questions have been raised in the past regarding your topic. Write them out, and have an answer ready. Have your practice audience throw questions at you during rehearsal.

According to Deborah Tannen, Ph.D., in her book *You Just Don't Understand*, men ask more questions and will be the first to raise their hand. They will also ask longer, more in-depth questions.

When a hand is raised, acknowledge the questioner by calling him or her by name (if you can see a name tag), and look the questioner in the eye, listen carefully to the entire question without second-guessing, then repeat the question or rephrase it so others can hear what was asked. Rephrasing ensures you understand the question. Repeating it gives you a few seconds to form an answer. It is important also to repeat the question if you are being recorded so that the question is heard on the tape.

Make your answers brief, and don't include extraneous information. Don't make another speech to show how much you know. Avoid getting involved in a two-person conversation, or letting one person dominate the question and answer period. Don't allow two people to take over the session with their own agenda. Others will lose interest or become angry.

Acknowledge everyone in the room who has a question—time permitting—and treat all questions with respect. Don't interrupt the questioner before she has had time to finish. Don't favor one side of the room over the other. Ask the program coordinator to help recognize audience members with questions.

If a question is asked on a topic you'll be covering later, say you appreciate the question, but you'll defer the question until that time. Should a question be asked while you're speaking, finish with your point, mark your place so you know where you left off, and then respond to the question. And finally, always thank the audience for their participation.

Handling Difficult Questions. Problems can arise when opening the floor to questions. Sooner or later you're going to meet an audience with difficult questions. Keep cool when handling them. As the TV commercial says, "Never let them see you sweat."

• The multiphased or complex question. Divide the question and answer it in parts, or you may choose to select only one part of the question and focus on it.

• The off-the-wall, silly, or embarrassing question. Whoever said there is no such thing as a stupid question never sat in one of my audiences. Be courteous, tactful, and always diplomatic. Remain in control while trying not to laugh, turn red, or shake your head as you answer. Handle the question and questioner with finesse, never a put-down. A callous remark will discourage the honest questioner who might wonder if his or her question might also be considered silly.

• The testing question. There will be those who feel compelled to test you because you're a woman. They know the answer, but want to find out how much you know and see how you respond. Some people think they know the answer and will ask a question anyway just for assurance.

Two techniques you can try in answering these kinds of questions are: 1. Turn the question back to the audience. When someone asks a question, paraphrase it and ask another member of the audience to answer the question, getting the audience involved at the same time. 2. Turn the question back to the person asking the question. "That's a good question, John. What do you think can be done about the violence in our schools?" I do this whenever I feel the questioner is testing me or has been a general pain in the derriere.

• The nonquestion. Some people with many years of living experience like to ramble on about what they did, when they did it, how they did it, and why. They don't have a question, but will waste your time with their exposition. Don't let this happen. In a courteous manner, take control of the situation. Interrupt the talker as soon as you see he or she doesn't have a question. Simply ask, "Do you have a question?" Others in the audience will be silently asking the same thing. Take control, or your audience could become resentful of their time being wasted on someone whom they didn't come to hear.

• The hostile question. There is a difference between a hostile question and a challenging question. A person may want more information or have preconceptions about your proposal. Clarification may be his or her goal, but hasn't thought how to phrase the question more gently. Questions such as, "Where did you get your facts?" "How can your proposal work here?" or "What evidence do you have?" may seem hostile and put you on the spot, but these questions reflect honest dialogue. Don't take them as hostile. Think beyond the question and ask yourself, "What does the person really want to know?" Not every question is an attempt to challenge you.

What is meant by a hostile question? Any question or comment that is directed at you, your beliefs, or lifestyle, phrased in a negative way about sex, race, and religion can be suspect. Questions such as, "How can you 'waltz in here in that dress' and expect us to buy into what you say?" The words in quotes indicate the root of the hostility: You are a woman.

When asked a question such as this, rephrase it and omit any loaded words and say, "Do I understand you to say, you need more information?" Sidestep the underlying meaning and never let them get to you. Stand firm in your purpose and you'll show them you aren't going to be intimidated.

If a question is a direct attack on you or your character and not the subject being discussed, decline to answer. The rest of the audience will understand and appreciate that you didn't take on a question that could lead to a verbal confrontation.

• The persistent questioner. If the same person is constantly waving a hand in the air to be recognized, not allowing others to ask questions, turn off the persistent questioner by placing a psychological distance between the two of you. Drop eye contact and shift your body away from the individual.

Some people don't listen. You can always tell by the questions they ask. You spent ten minutes going over a point, and now you have to repeat the information because "Joe Cool" wasn't listening. What do you do? It's hard to maintain a sense of humor when this happens, and you can't chastise the person. You can think it, but never take your frustrations out on the audience. I always say something like, "I'm glad you asked that because that point is worth repeating." Then repeat the answer briefly.

It never hurts to repeat information (if you have time). By repeating an answer you do several things. You haven't embarrassed the questioner; you maintained control; and you enlightened someone else who might not have been listening.

When you see that one question has led to another, and the second question has gone off course, bring the focus back to the original question or refer to a previously made statement and then move on. You must cut off the questions when they begin to go astray.

I've had women tell me they were concerned about getting sidetracked. I tell them, as long as you and the audience are on the same train, don't worry. A question asked in the middle of your presentation can cause you to digress. Don't let this worry you. If you have time, let the audience know you are digressing by saying, "This is off the subject, but you bring up an interesting or important point." Then go on to make a brief statement. Be sure to pull the speech back on track after you have finished your additional comment.

The Q & A Session. Every informative speech should include a question and answer session. In most cases, you will have an audience eager to ask questions, but there will also be times when you get no response to, "Are there any questions?" If this happens—and it often does when people are too shy to ask the first question—ask the first question yourself by saying, "I'm often asked, where can I find that book?" Give the answer and then ask if there are any other questions; or you can have a few prepared questions given to the chairperson ahead of time. But make sure the chairperson isn't a comedian. I heard a story once where a speaker gave several prepared questions to a friend in the audience to get the ball rolling. The first question was asked and the speaker responded cleverly, and the audience laughed. The friend asked the second question and again the speaker answered, this time bringing huge laughter. Then the friend stood and inquired, "What was that third question you wanted me to ask?"

Don't worry if no one responds immediately. Give them time to generate questions. Some people are reluctant to speak up for fear others might think their question is dumb or a waste of time. Compliment the questioner. Comments such as "I'm glad you asked that" encourage others to participate. Avoid complimenting everyone, however, or you'll begin to sound insincere.

A couple of points to remember: When answering a complex question, always ask if you have answered the question to the satisfaction of the questioner.

Let the audience be funny. If someone pipes up with a remark that brings laugher, laugh along. Give the person a big smile, make a check mark in the air, and say, "That's one for the lady in the blue dress." If they are really funny, make a gesture for them to take the microphone and say, "You're really good at this. Ever consider going on stage as a comic?" or "I'm speaking to the Rotary Club next week. I could use you in my audience." Let them know you think they helped you with your presentation.

Some Q and A sessions become a lively exchange of information and ideas. I find answering questions fun, but it's easy to lose track of the time. Again, ask the chairperson to help you stay on time by having her (or him) call an end to the question and answer session if she sees you're running over. Draw the Q and A session to a close by saying something like, "I have time for only two more questions." Or conclude the session with, "That's all the time we have for questions. If you would like to talk with me afterward, I'll be happy to answer your remaining questions then." Never let the Q and A wind down until there are no questions left. Always leave them wanting more.

I suggest that you place the Q and A just before your conclusion. Always have the last word so you can leave the audience satisfied that everything you have said is complete.

If you say you'll be around after the presentation for questions, don't rush off. Make yourself available for a one-on-one with individual members of the audience. Some people keep their questions to themselves, afraid to speak up, or maybe their question is of a personal nature and they didn't feel comfortable talking about it in front of the group. Remaining afterward gives them a chance to share their ideas and ask the questions they couldn't ask in front of others.

It's also good for business. If they liked what they heard and saw, they may ask you back again. If you are speaking on behalf of your company, you may be expected to network with prospective clients.

What to Say When You Don't Know the Answer. It's perfectly okay not to know the answer to every possible question. But don't begin your answer by saying, "Well, ah." I've already discussed why, and I don't want to beat that horse anymore, but beginning your answer with those words makes you sound hesitant and indecisive.

If you don't know the answer, say so. You can't possibly know everything. Never apologize for not knowing the answer. Be up front about it. Don't hedge or try to evade the question and don't try to bluff your way through. It never works.

Never leave a question unanswered. When you get hit with a question for which you don't know the answer—and your subject is not of a serious nature—you could say something like, "That's a good question and I wish I knew the answer." If you scratch your head at the same time you'll probably provoke laughter. The audience will appreciate that you're human and willing to admit your failings, but always let the questioner know that you're interested in finding the answer and will do so. Tell her that you will get back to her with an answer, then do it. If you are speaking out of town, getting back to someone may be an additional expense, but it's worth the effort in the long run when your reputation is at stake.

When you don't know the answer, but know of someone in the audience who does, pass the question to that person. Say, "Lois, you've had experience in that area. What do you think?"

Don't put Lois on the spot. Make sure she doesn't have a problem speaking up.

Allow yourself a little extra time to think about an answer. Arrange to have a glass of water on the shelf below the lectern. Take a sip and collect your thoughts. The pause gives you time to think without looking as though you are groping for an answer.

DISTRIBUTING HANDOUTS

When do you hand them out? The answer depends on the type of speech given and the speaking situation. If you want your audience to follow along with you as you explain information, you need to pass around the handouts at the beginning of your presentation. Handing out reading material just before you begin to speak, however, can cause a distraction as everyone shuffles through the pages, reading ahead while you're speaking. This is not the ideal situation, and most speakers try to avoid handing out information ahead of time whenever possible, but sometimes it's necessary. I haven't found a satisfactory solution to not having the audience look at the handout. Asking them not to read ahead just doesn't work.

Make sure the audience is following along with you. If you've skipped over an item, let the audience know you're skipping it and why. Don't leave them on number four while you are talking about number six. Wait until everyone has turned to the correct page, pause until you see everyone has stopped turning pages. Say something like, "Now, is everyone on page two? Good, we can begin." If you spy someone turning ahead, you can make a joke about it by saying, "I see Joe is so anxious to know what we are going to learn next, he has already read the next page." Kid around with your audience in an informal situation or when you know your audience can take the jabs.

Get assistance with handouts. Make arrangements for distribution ahead of time. If you have people sitting to your right and left, divide the handouts into two stacks and give them to the people in the front and let them pass them back. Don't try to pass them out yourself. You'll waste time, and half of the audience won't hear you if you continue to talk.

If you are going to distribute the handouts at the end of your speech, don't let them sit exposed to the audience. The audience will wonder if the material is for them, what's in the handout, when they'll get it, and if the notes they are taking are in the handout. They don't need this distraction.

And finally, make enough handouts for everyone.

MAKING A GRACEFUL EXIT

The speech is finally over. The many long hours of preparation and practice have paid off. The audience loved you and they're applauding your success. You stand basking in the warm fuzzies of the applause. Now what?

I've seen women so relieved to reach the conclusion of the speech they let out a huge sigh of relief and practically sat before finishing their last words. Or they stood looking to the right, then to the left, as if looking for an escape hatch. When no one came to the lectern to shake their hand, they gathered their notes, smiled, and awkwardly walked off the stage. That's not the impression you want to leave with your audience.

Wait, there's a better way.

Let the audience know you appreciate their applause. Actors love curtain calls. They'll stand and take bow after bow until the stage manager finally says "enough." It's the actor's way of saying thank you for coming and enjoying the performance. Actors bathe in the warmth of the applause. I recommend you do the same. Stand for a few seconds—although it may seem longer—and smile at the audience as they applaud you. Don't rush offstage.

I like applause and I milk it for all its worth. I stay at the lectern until somebody comes to rescue me. It's my old Toastmasters training, I suppose, that says never leave the lectern unattended. But if no one shows up, keep smiling and take your seat.

10

Special Concerns
for Women at the Lectern

We must overcome the notion that we must be regular. . . .
It robs you of the chance to be extraordinary and leads
you to the mediocre.

Uta Hagen, *Respect for Acting*

Verbal communication in today's business world is more important than ever. People are measured by how well they express their opinions, discuss and analyze problems, and share ideas. For women, these factors are even more critical because of the long history of narrow focused ideas of where "a woman's place" was supposed to be. For centuries women, like children, were to be seen, not heard, especially in politics and decisions involving the church. The very idea of a woman expressing her thoughts, ideas, and beliefs drew scorn and condemnation.

Those antiquated views are gone, but left behind is a stigma sewn into the fabric of our society that says women still don't have anything important to say. Here are just a few examples of how men view women:

"When a man dies, the last thing that moves is his heart; in a woman, her tongue" (George Chapman, *The Widow's Tears*).

"Generally speaking, women are" (*More Playboy's Party Jokes*).

"If a woman could talk out of two sides of her mouth at the same time, a great deal would be said on both sides" (George D. Prentice, Journalist).

"You are a woman. You must never speak what you think, your words must contradict your thoughts, but your actions may contradict your words" (William Congreve, *Love for Love*).

"Women never use their intelligence—except when they need to prop up their intuition" (Jacques Deval, *News Summaries*).

"A woman's preaching is like a dog walking on his hind legs. It is not done well; but you are surprised to find it done at all" (Samuel Johnson, *Boswell's Life*).

"The reason there are so few women after-dinner speakers is because few can wait that long" (author unknown).

"Women are nothing but machines for producing children" (Napoleon I).

"One who never opens her mouth unless she has nothing to say" (Anon).

The erroneous belief that girls *can't* do or say anything important was hammered into them at a young age. The results are low self-esteem and self-doubt, causing women to feel inferior and sabotage their own success.

Eleanor Roosevelt said, "No one can make you feel inferior without your consent."

THE CREDIBILITY PROBLEM

Even with the great strides and advancements women have made in the past decades, we are often perceived as weak negotiators, poor problem solvers, indecisive decision makers, and frivolous money managers.

Dee Dee Myers, former press secretary to the president, said that women in Washington face extra burdens because of their gender. "Washington is still, and politics and government generally are still, very much dominated by men," she said. "I think it is always more difficult, or often more difficult, for women to have the same authority and the same credibility that men have."

The perceived abilities of women as public speakers also falls far behind that of men. Men have always been viewed as the authority, the ones with all the facts. They express themselves with clear-cut logic. Women express their ideas emotionally.

Women fail as communicators because (1) they are perceived by society as lacking anything important to say, and (2) because they don't believe in their own abilities.

Judith C. Tingley, Ph.D., says, "The structure of men's communication is generally viewed as more powerful than that of women's communication. When a man and woman speaker of the same skills, experience, and credentials each deliver identical speeches to similar audiences, the male is remembered more clearly and fully, and he is seen as more credible than the female speaker" (*The Toastmaster*, May 1990).

I have discovered that successful women have gathered their courage and have taken the necessary steps to prepare for today's challenges. They have done their homework and paid their dues. They are in positions of power as heads of companies and government organizations. Women are forming their own companies, forging paths in areas unheard of twenty years ago.

According to Patricia Aburdene, author of *Megatrends for Women*, women are challenging and overturning the status quo and recasting social, economic, and political trends of today.

Women are making headway in the '90s. We know and understand the necessity of good communication skills, and are fine-tuning our ability to speak in public. We *are* able to communicate our thoughts and ideas clearly and persuasively, and are doing so every day.

There is no easy one-step miracle method for overcoming the problem of how society views women, but there are steps a woman can take to begin building credibility on the speaking platform. It takes time to undo years of self-doubt and to build self-confidence. Success in anything requires work and persistence. Unfortunately, for some women, the problem of low self-esteem and lack of confidence will always exist.

Some women really do have a credibility problem. A woman confided in me that she had to give a speech to an audience of college professors and was scared to death. "I only went to high school. My grades weren't very good. My grammar is awful. They'll know I'm not very smart," she told me.

It took some work to build her confidence, but I made her understand that those professors got where they are by investing a lot of time listening to people. I convinced her she had special knowledge on a subject that those professors wanted in order to make their lives better. I made her see that they were on her side. They wanted her to succeed, because the better she was at relating information, the more they would benefit.

The members of your audience have needs they believe will be fulfilled by listening to you. They want you to do your best so they can learn new information. They may need the information for their jobs, for the enjoyment of a hobby, or to solve a personal problem. Maybe they need to relax, and your speech satisfies that need. They are there to learn from you, not to criticize, judge, or ridicule. Don't allow self-doubt to get in your way.

Ways Women Can Establish Credibility

You say no one knows who you are. The audience has never heard of you. The only thing they know about you is your name printed on the program. How can you establish your credibility in the eyes of your audience?

Your attitude toward your topic, willingness to share information, and the enthusiasm, respect, and compassion you exhibit toward your audience, combined with the trust and confidence you generate, greatly influences the level of respect the audience gives you in return.

To establish and increase your credibility at the beginning and throughout your presentation follow these suggestions:

• Write your own introduction. If no one knows you or what you do, they'll sit thinking, Who is this woman? What's her experience and background? How much does she really know about this topic? They'll wonder if you're worth their time sitting and listening to you. A good introduction answers those questions as it builds your credibility.

Let the world know who you are. Toot your own horn. Don't get a "case of the modesties." Your introduction should answer why you are speaking to this audience and why you are speaking on this subject at this time. It should explain why you were selected to speak on this subject, what makes you the authority, and what your experience is relating to the topic.

As you write your introduction, tell how you became interested in the subject. Include what research you've conducted, the degrees you hold, and any distinguishing accomplishments that make you the expert. You will also want to state your job experience, organization affiliations, and occupation if it enhances your image.

The idea is to build and boost yourself in the eyes of the audience. As you write your introduction, include your name in the opening, in the body, and in the conclusion.

• Present yourself in a competent manner. Competent means you know your stuff and you show it by the way you walk to the lectern. Be confident, organized, with butterflies under control. Smile, you're ready to make a great presentation.

• Adopt a friendly, personable manner. How do you feel listening to somebody who acts superior? Do they seem unreachable? If you want your audience to feel comfortable, make them feel you truly like talking to them and are happy to be there. Smile often with warmth and sincerity. Look the audience in the eyes.

• Speak with authority. You know your subject. You have confidence in your ability to present that information. Don't allow your voice or what you say to betray you. Phrases and words such as, *I think, maybe, I believe, I'm not sure about this, but . . .* , diminish your effectiveness. Use language that is direct and precise. Say what you have to say without hedging. Be straightforward.

- Present verifiable facts backed by testimony, quotes, and visual support. So maybe you aren't the expert. You haven't spent years in the trenches doing research. You didn't do the laboratory experiments. But you can report the findings of others. Quote experts in the field. As you present the main points of your speech, support everything you say with solid evidence that backs your claim. Give all the facts. State where you got the information and be sure to give credit to the experts for their work. Every time you introduce an expert into your talk you add credibility to your presentation.

- Be on time. You never know when something will happen on the road that will cause a delay. But how will the program coordinator know you're stuck in traffic? I attended a meeting recently where this happened. The program chair could only shrug her shoulders and say she had no idea where the speaker was or if he would show. We went on. But in the back of my mind, I kept wondering what happened to the speaker. What a distraction that was. If you're going to be late, call.

- Present the best-quality visual aids and handouts possible. I'll say this again: Your visual aids are a direct representation of you and your standards. If they're sloppy, it says you don't care enough to take the extra time and effort to do your best for your audience. Your handouts could be kept around for a long time and used as resources and shared with others. What impression will be formed about you from your visual aids and handouts?

- Dress appropriately. There is an old rule of thumb that says you should dress in the same manner or one step better than your audience. Your attire should fit the speaking situation. But most of all, what you wear must match your message and conform to what the audience expects. A business meeting or executive briefing calls for business dress, while more casual attire would be acceptable for a speech given to an avant garde group. Wearing the wrong clothes for a speech can make or break your credibility. The important thing is to look professional, confident, and comfortable.

- Above all—act professional! Even if you aren't a professional speaker, you can act like one. Be professional from the inside out. You never know who's in your audience who might be looking for someone as confident as you to work for them.

Credibility Killers

You will be destined to ruin a speech and destroy your credibility if you do any of the following:

1. *Neglect to walk your talk.* Elizabeth Jeffries, professional speaker and author on leadership and personal performance, says you must "walk your talk." She means that your appearance, attitude, and integrity must match your message. The length of your hair, the height of the heel of your shoe, and the amount of makeup you use must suit your presentation.

2. *Be negative.* Examine your motives for making the speech. Ask yourself why you want to talk to this audience. Do you see making a speech as an avenue for personal development and success? Do you enjoy sharing information so that others may learn and grow? Or are you doing it because your boss told you to? Either way, a negative attitude hangs out there like dingy laundry on the clothesline.

3. *Present irrelevant information.* How many times have you sat listening to a speaker and wondered what the information had to do with the topic? The speaker either wanted to fill in time or didn't have a clue how to give a speech. Too much information can be as bad as not enough, especially if the information lends no special insight into the topic.

4. *Put down other people's products or services.* Your product or service may be the best around, but you don't have to put others down in order to build yours up.

5. *Make excuses or apologize for your presentation.* Some speakers feel if they make excuses for not being well prepared it pardons them from doing a good job. When you tell the audience you didn't have time to prepare as well as you should have, you're telling them you don't care about them, or whether or not you present a good speech.

6. *Misrepresent your topic.* A high standard of ethics is critical in maintaining credibility. State your intentions. Never lie to your audience or violate their trust. Never exaggerate, slant, dis-

tort, or manipulate the facts. Never suppress key information in order to make your ideas sound better. And never give the impression that the information is the result of your own research when it isn't. That's plagiarism and it's the cardinal sin. It's perfectly okay to use someone else's words, but you *must* give them attribution.

7. *Use poor grammar.* If you're unsure about your grammar, ask someone to help you or buy a good grammar book. The old standby, *The Elements of Style*, by Strunk and White is used and recommended by many writers. The book is small, inexpensive, and can be found in libraries and most bookstores.

8. *Use politically incorrect language.* It's almost impossible to keep up with who wants to be called what. Indians are no longer Indians, but Native Americans. Negroes are no longer black, but African American. People once called "handicapped" or "disabled" are now "physically challenged."

Extreme feminists are offended by any reference to the word *man* in words such as *chairman* or *mankind.* For years, terms such as *schitzo* and *senile* were used to point a finger at those who acted differently. Now those terms offend.

The situation has gone from silly to crazy. Tall people are vertically enhanced and short people are vertically challenged. A thief is a noncompensated shopper. A bald man is follicle challenged. Being ugly means having a facial deficiency.

Keeping up with the trends will take work if you want to be politically and socially correct. If you don't know what term is currently being used, find out. Call the association affiliated with the group you want to mention, and make the correct reference.

9. *Tell off-color jokes and use inappropriate language that degrades sex, religion, race, or nationality.* Never be guilty of this.

10. *Appear to have had too much to drink.* You're nervous and a few belts of Jack Daniel's calm your nerves. It also ruins your reputation if you appear drunk.

11. *Present a sloppy appearance.* Murphy must have something against coffee, sauces, and gravy because they don't stay in the cup or on the plate. Accidents happen and can be excused. The kind of sloppy appearance I'm talking about is

poor grooming, hair in need of a shampooing, or wrinkled and soiled clothing.

12. *Disclose a personal problem.* You may have dust bunnies under your bed, but unless you're trying to be like Erma Bombeck, too much personal disclosure can ruin your credibility. I once heard a woman tell what a bad housekeeper she was; how two weeks' worth of laundry was piled up, dishes had been left in the sink for days, and how the mess the dog made was still in the middle of the floor. I sat in disbelief that not only could someone live like that, but that she would admit it. Her purpose was to illustrate how busy we become and how things get out of control. But in my eyes, her credibility was ruined.

13. *Have a weak, ineffectual voice.* I have already covered how to use the voice effectively, but one more thing needs to be said. No matter how great you look, how well prepared, or how knowledgeable you are, if your voice sounds weak, you'll come across as lacking authority.

Many women have soft voices that project a soothing effect. And although pleasant sounding, it is not always an asset. Lilyan Wilder, speech consultant, says many women don't get ahead because their voices lack authority. "They speak in faint, breathy voices, while men boom," she said. When following a male speaker with a strong booming voice, the woman's voice sounds weak by comparison. If you're trying to compete or persuade, the strength of your voice can affect your overall presentation. Save the soft, demure, powder puff voice for the bedroom.

14. *Play the soubrette.* Gushing with girlish enthusiasm makes you look immature, naive, and unprofessional. Putting on the cutesy little-girl act and giggling has no place at the lectern.

15. *Have a regional accent.* If you have an accent and are speaking to a group that shares the same accent, yours won't be noticed. Take that accent outside that region and you'll receive mixed reactions—everything from "Isn't she darling" to ugly prejudice. If your accent is so heavy that it impedes the listener's ability to understand, you'll need to work on changing the way you talk.

16. *Rattle on and on about yourself and your accomplishments.* No one likes a braggart. Bring yourself into your speech only as an example to help others learn from your experience.

17. *Exceed your allotted time.* I'll repeat this: Don't run overtime. If you're scheduled to speak for thirty minutes, be darn sure you don't speak for forty. Stay within your specified time limit, give or take two minutes.

18. *Use disclaimers and qualifiers that dilute and weaken your effectiveness.* Pam Zarit, a media trainer and president of Pam Zarit Communications in New York, says avoid "hedge words" and tag lines. Rather than saying "I hope you will like this proposal" which sounds weak, rephrase to say, "I know you will accept this proposal."

Women tend to end sentences with tag lines such as "Isn't that right?" "Okay?" "Don't you think?"—which sound as if they need the audience's permission. Then there's the qualifier, "I'm just a secretary or housewife." There is never a "just" to anything you are or do.

Words and phrases such as *I think, maybe, sort of, I don't have all the facts, but . . . , I'm not sure, but . . . , pretty good, probably,* make you look indecisive. Know exactly what you want to say and how you wish to say it.

19. *Use timid, girlish, or coy mannerisms or gestures.* Constantly tilting or cocking your head and pointing the toe of your shoe in the air can be interpreted as coy or submissive. It's inappropriate, especially while making an executive briefing. Shrugging your shoulders in a cutesy manner is unbusinesslike in today's business environment.

20. *Cry.* Choking with emotion makes an audience uneasy. They will feel helpless and embarrassed.

Handling the Male Heckler

They're out there, and sooner or later, you're going to run into one—the heckler, the troublemaker, the jerk. This is the person who feels compelled to disrupt your presentation. If you were a comic in a nightclub like Don Rickles, you might expect to be heckled. You would welcome the chance to banter with the audience. But in any other speaking situation the heckler is not welcome. Dealing with hecklers is a specialty of Don Rickles, but for you, a woman, they're a nuisance and, for some, can be devastating. Some men like to give a woman a difficult time by exerting their self-imposed superiority. Nevertheless, you must deal with them because they never go away on their own. Maintaining and using your wit is the only answer.

In the 1992 campaign, George Bush didn't win many votes when he yelled to a heckler to shut up. A comment such as that may be what you would like to say, but you must remain composed and in control and, above all, show respect to all members of the audience, no matter what you think of their behavior.

You have many options for handling the heckler or troublemaker. Consultant and trainer Judy Zinn believes that most men are willing to listen to a woman. Whenever possible, she solves any problem with male hecklers by asking for their opinion. "They like to give their opinions. This lowers their defensiveness," she said.

Dorothy Leeds, president of Organizational Technologies, Inc., says when dealing with a difficult subject, expect a hostile audience. Begin your session by asking audience members to state their name, company, and title before they ask a question. Leeds says that many people don't like to volunteer personal information, especially if they aren't acquainted with others in the group. Requesting they respond in this manner cuts down on the number of unfriendly questions you might be asked.

Use humor to defuse caustic remarks. The audience will enjoy it and the heckler will be deflated in a nice way. Don't reply with sarcasm. Sarcasm is a an excuse for honest communication. A man using sarcasm would appear cool, witty, and on top of things, but a woman will be viewed as snide or snippy. You never want to lower yourself to the level of the heckler. Suppose someone in the audience makes the comment, "City council is a bunch of jerks." You could respond with, "I understand some people do feel that way." This is not the time to ask him to explain his comment, because he will, and you run the risk of losing control. Never egg on a heckler by disagreeing with him unless you are prepared for a battle. That's what he wants. Don't provoke a negative response. Don't reply to outrageous statements or questions with comments such as, "You're wrong" or "That's not correct."

Whenever possible, ignore the comment. Some hecklers are smart enough to recognize this as a sign to shut up. The audience will appreciate that you didn't encourage the heckler and waste their time while you parried with him.

The heckler is another reason to ask your contact person if the audience will be drinking. Some service organizations are notorious for their rowdy activities at conventions. Knowing they might be drunk gives you the opportunity to ask your contact person to act as sergeant at arms and stand by to escort the heckler from the room, if necessary.

Most importantly, you must remain in control while at the lectern. The audience will look to you to handle the situation quickly and effectively without becoming flustered.

Six Types of Troublemakers

1. *The Silent Disagreer.* These are the folks who sit in the back of the room, shake their head, and roll their eyes at everything you say. Never allow a member of your audience to intimidate you. It's best to ignore the minority in your audience who send negative feedback. Concentrate on the majority who are listening attentively.

2. *The Nay-sayer.* Ever hear, "We tried doing that before and it didn't work." I love that comment. It contains a host of negativity. I approach this troublemaker with my own who, where, what, when, and how. "When did you try this? Who was responsible for the planning? How was the program conducted? Where did you do this? What media did you use?" By the time I'm through bombarding him with my questions, he's deflated, realizing there could have been many reasons why his project failed. Then I set into motion my proposal by explaining how the project *will* work.

3. *The Constant Talker.* David A. Peoples, author of *Presentations Plus,* suggests that you move closer to the troublemaker

and keep strong eye contact until you are standing right in front of him. Because you are standing and he is sitting, you have the dominant position.

4. *Mr. Expert-on-Everything.* This guy never hesitates to inform you that he knows more than you and can say it better. He'll add comments during your speech to let you know that you haven't completely covered every detail. He'll preface his remarks with phrases such as, "My experience has been . . ." or "As an expert in the field of . . ." or "With my twenty years in business . . ." My response is to acknowledge the person by saying, "You seem to be knowledgeable about this subject. I would like to hear what you have to say. Perhaps we could talk after the meeting." You're setting guidelines and placing the person on notice that his remarks are useful, but only in the context which you are willing to accept. He'll get the message.

5. *The Verbal Disagreer.* You can't please everyone, and may find one to two people who want to flex their muscles by announcing that you're wrong. Don't let them. Simply say, "You may have a valid point, and if you want to discuss this further, we can continue this at the break or after the meeting." Don't waste time with folks who don't add positively to the program. Give your energy to those who appreciate it.

6. *The Buttinski.* This guy is a second cousin to Mr. Expert-on-Everything. He'll constantly butt in and add his comments and/or suggestions to what you say. He's annoying. Let him know you appreciate his comments and ask him to hold on to his thoughts until you have finished, otherwise you'll never get home for dinner.

Dealing With the Troublemaker

It's possible that a person isn't really a troublemaker, but only comes off sounding like one. Search to see if the person has a hidden agenda. The comments made could be just the manner in which the person communicates. His sarcasm may be a failed attempt to be funny. Sandy Linver, author of *Speak Easy*, says, "Take into account the whole person, not only the words he says but the sound of his voice, his facial expression, and his body posture. If you simply respond to the words of the question or comment, you may not have dealt with the source of the hostility or disagreement." You may also miss his meaning altogether.

If you realize that the comment was an attempt to hassle you and the situation escalates, it's important to remember that you don't have to put up with rude behavior. Frederick Gilbert, Ph.D., author and president of Frederick Gilbert Associates, Inc., a speech training and consulting firm, offers these suggestions for handling the troublemaker:

1. *Stop talking.* The unexpected silence breeds silence. If that doesn't work . . .

2. *Walk closer to the troublemaker.* Often a physical closeness sets up a psychological barrier and places you in a dominant position. If that doesn't work . . .

3. *Stop the program briefly and ask the talker to be quiet.* If that doesn't work . . .

4. *Confront the person privately during a break and enlist his cooperation.* If that doesn't work . . .

5. *Confront the person publicly during the program and ask him to stop talking or leave.* Finally, if that doesn't work . . .

6. *End the program early.* Remember, you don't have to put up with a rude person.

WHAT SHOULD I WEAR?

What you wear while speaking is as important as what you say when it comes to establishing your credibility and feeling good about yourself. Pauline Frederick, broadcast news analyst, said, "When a man gets up to speak, people listen, then look. When a woman gets up, people look, then, if they like what they see, they listen." Like it or not, we form opinions and place a great importance—consciously or subconsciously—on others' "image."

Consider these guidelines:

• If you buy a new outfit for the presentation, a word of warning: Wear it first. I read a newspaper column that said buying a new outfit would help you feel better about yourself and help you control nervousness. I don't agree with that theory for two reasons. First, no superficial cover-up, such as a new dress, can substitute for proper preparation; and second, new clothing, if not worn and rehearsed in, can become a nightmare when you get to the lectern and discover the skirt is too tight after eating, the jacket doesn't allow for large gestures, or there is no place to pin a microphone.

Wearing a new outfit isn't going to enhance your credibility if the clothes are ill-fitting, making you feel uncomfortable. The audience will notice your discomfort and possibly misinterpret it as nervousness.

• Wear clothing of high quality that reflects your personal taste and style and that flatters your body type. Watch what other successful women are wearing.

• When wearing two-piece outfits, always wear the jacket, preferably with shoulder pads.

• Avoid sleeveless and low-cut dresses or blouses with buttons in front.

• Wear comfortable clothes with a quiet elegance that command authority and make you feel good about yourself. Wear clothes that match your presentation. Ask yourself, "Do my clothes send a positive impression?"

• Consider the hemline. Hem lengths change with each fashion trend. Skirt lengths that tip the top of the knee may look fine while standing, but how high does the skirt ride up while sitting? If you're seated in front of the audience as a panel member with no covering on the table, the audience will have a good look at your legs. Help keep your audience focused on what you're saying, not on your anatomy.

• Choose clothes that travel well without wrinkling. It's a good idea to carry a travel iron; hotels usually charge for the use of theirs.

• Keep in mind that you may be using a clip-on microphone. The lapel of a suit jacket works well for holding the clip, but clipping the microphone onto a soft material will pinch the cloth and cause it to sag. The clip can also snag the cloth. Wireless microphones require that you wear a battery pack or transmitter. I suggest you select a suit with a long jacket that will hide the equipment.

What About Color?

The most often asked question about clothes is, "What color is best?" For years I believed that dark, conservative colors were the only option. I want to debunk that notion right now. Although wearing a conservative dark suit or dress is appropriate and expected in some speaking situations, such as when speaking to bankers, I suggest you wear color in most circumstances.

Recently at a conference, I saw two women on a panel speak to a group of professional businesswomen. One wore a soft rose knit suit. The other woman wore a conservative dull olive green suit with a tan blouse. As I watched the two women, I couldn't help notice how my eyes kept following the woman in the rose-colored suit. It was stunning, making her exciting to watch. Seeing her on stage made me realize the rule of wearing only dark conservative colors while making a speech was probably a carryover from days when men wore only one kind of suit appropriate for speech making—dark.

Don't be afraid to wear soft, deep, rich colors of blue, emerald green, red, teal, and burgundy for sparkle and excitement, but avoid pastels that are weak and lack authority.

Just as color adds power to visual aids, colorful clothing adds sparkle to you, holds the audience's interest, and subtly says you have good taste and are conscious of how you look. Stay away from gaudy colors and designs. Avoid multicolored plaids, stripes, large prints, and floral designs—and tiger-skin patterns are definitely out.

I'm not advocating that you go out and buy a new wardrobe of colorful dresses and suits just for a speaking engagement. You can dress up dark gray, green, brown, or blue outfits by adding a colorful blouse, scarf, or shawl collar. Study your personal coloring and determine what color looks best on you. Wear colors that compliment your skin and hair coloring.

Find out what kind of wall or color of curtain will be behind you, such as yellow or red brick, purple curtain or gold club banner, so you can coordinate the color of your outfit to it.

Additional tips for looking good:

• To wear or not to wear eyeglasses. Sandra didn't like wearing glasses; she said they made her look frumpy. But because she couldn't see two feet in front of her nose, she squinted, screwing her face into an expression that made her look as if she had just smelled a five-days-dead fish.

Some say glasses hide your eyes and lessen the strength of eye contact. If the alternative is tripping or falling off the stage because you can't see, wear your glasses.

Contact lenses are a solution to conventional glasses, but they, too, can create problems. One speaker told me that her lenses always dried when speaking in hotels and conference centers because the air was dry, irritating her eyes and making them red.

• Wear comfortable, quiet shoes. Shoes must be comfortable, especially if you are standing for any length of time. Avoid shoes with metal tips or cleats that make noise when you walk across the stage. The same goes for squeaky shoes. Carpeted floors can't conceal a talking shoe. Shoes should be dark in color. Is that a hard and fast rule? I say it's about as solid as they get. I am always distracted by shoes that are a different color other than the hem of the skirt or dress. That goes for the shade of hosiery, too. Both should be neutral or dark in color. You want the audience's attention on your face and hands. Everything from the waist down should be diminished. One last point about shoes—make sure they are polished and free from mud and grime. Check the heels. Are they in need of repair?

• Watch the makeup. You want to look pretty—don't we all. Makeup helps hide a multitude of years, but the amount of makeup you apply should be subtle. Wear a light shade of eye shadow if you wear glasses. Lighter shades draw attention to your eyes. Added lip gloss brightens your overall look. There are many consultants today who can help select the shades and colors just right for you. Take their advice.

• Take care of your hands. They're a visual aid. Pamper your-self and get a manicure.

• Wear a hair style that flatters your face, that is easy to care for, and isn't a distraction. Keep your bangs out of your eyes and make sure your part is straight. I sat watching a speaker whose part looked like the crooked creek that runs behind our house. I don't remember much about her speech, but I sure remember that jagged part in her hair. The audience will be see-ing you from different angles, so check your hair from the back and sides as well as the front.

Things to avoid:

• Hair clips and bows. Find a hairstyle that can be worn without the aid of clips, bows, or other devices; they're dis-tracting and can come undone.

• Fancy clips and buttons on shoes and stockings with fancy designs.

• Bright fingernail color. Wear a neutral or light muted shade of polish.

• Flashy jewelry. Keep jewelry to a minimum. Dangling ear-rings that sway back and forth and charm bracelets that clang against the lectern are distracting. Accent pins on the lapel are acceptable, if small.

• Ruffles around the face and slits in the skirt.

• Purse. Is there any reason to carry your purse to the lectern? I can't think of one good reason, unless it's used as a prop. Leave the purse under your chair or locked in the trunk of your car, but never take it with you to the lectern.

• Buttons on the cuff of your sleeve that can clatter against the lectern.

WHAT TO DO WHEN THINGS GO WRONG

We all have bad hair days, and some are worse than others, but making a speech is the time to put on a happy face and leave your problems on the doorstep, even when disaster strikes. Mak-ing a speech is like a performance, and no matter what happens, the show must go on. Even if you have prepared well, you may come upon a situation that would test the composure of a saint. Be ready to stretch your skills and make last-minute adjustments.

Audiences have long memories. They may not remember what you said a week after your speech, but they will remember how you lost your cool or became angry and upset when things didn't go the way you planned. When things go wrong, the audience will react the way you react. If you laugh it off, they will laugh. Become angry and they will become angry too, but not for the same reason. They will be angry because you didn't take command of the situation and solve the problem.

Many things that go wrong won't be your fault. Somebody else goofed, forgot, or didn't follow instructions. Be ready when this happens, and never let it throw you. I saw a speaker get upset because the room wasn't set up the way he wanted. He stormed around, yelling at the hotel staff and the conference chairperson. He could have easily pitched in and helped move the chairs and tables, but instead he acted as if everyone was there to please him. Fortunately, the audience hadn't arrived yet and wasn't witness to his tirade. But he made sure they knew about it during his speech. He came off looking like a professional jerk.

Think of all the things that could possibly go wrong while making your speech, write them down, then think of how you would handle the situation if it actually did happen. Anticipating and solving problems before they occur can save you hours of worry and make you look like a pro. Yes, plan for the worst. It probably won't happen, but you're prepared just in case.

That's Not the Introduction You Wrote. You wrote the introduction and gave it to the person who was supposed to introduce you, but for some unknown reason she bypassed your written introduction and introduced you with a cursory, "Our speaker today is Mary Jones."

You needed that introduction to set up your topic and prepare the audience for what you wanted to achieve. Now, you're left with nothing.

This won't happen often. Ninety-nine out of one hundred people will follow your instructions and read your introduction verbatim. Don't allow a no-introduction situation to throw you. Simply add to your opening remarks information the audience needs in order to have a better understanding of your topic and who you are.

Another Speaker Runs Overtime. I had this happen to me. I was scheduled to speak for fifty minutes and had prepared for a fifty-minute presentation. The speaker ahead of me was scheduled for a twenty-minute presentation. After thirty minutes, when she hadn't begun to slow down, I knew I was in trouble. I knew I couldn't give my full presentation because I would run over into lunch, and there is nothing worse than trying to talk to a group of hungry people who see food sitting on the buffet table just within reach. I quickly started to mentally slice and dice my presentation. What could I take out and still make the speech work? Standing in the back of the room, I shuffled through my visual aids and eliminated an entire section. I knew I could adjust my notes at the lectern.

Because of the time crunch the speaker created, the person making my introduction forgot to set up the overhead projector and screen and readjust the microphone before I arrived at the lectern. The situation had gone from chaotic to a nightmare. Realizing something had to be done and done quickly, I announced that since we had just heard such a wonderful speech, we deserved a stand-and-stretch break. This gave me the time needed to setup my visuals, adjust the microphone, and take a much-needed deep breath.

I presented my fifty-minute speech in twenty-five minutes, we had lunch on time, and everyone survived. Guess who was asked to come back and speak again and who wasn't?

That brings up another question. What can you cut out of your speech and still say what's needed? First, cut anecdotes. They add color to your speech and help to clarify your point, but do you need all of them? Next, eliminate visual aids. It may be that you just can't cut any of your speech and still have it make the same impact. If that's the case, the best thing you can do is not present your speech. It's better not to speak than to go ahead and do a bad job, but this would be the last resort.

Someone Changed the Room! You did everything right. You checked the room before planning your speech. You visualized it during practice. You were comfortable with the room. Everything was going to work just fine, and now somebody has gone and changed the room. Be prepared for last-minute changes, and adjust.

I attended a convention where the room for a very popular speaker's breakout session overflowed with an eager audience. The solution, of course, was to change the room to a bigger one to accommodate the crowd. But with the solution came another problem. A support pole sat in the middle of the room, creating a sightline problem. The speaker had planned to use overheads, but everyone seated near or to the rear of the pole couldn't see the screen. She quickly decided to eliminate the overheads all together. (This is another reason for never building your speech around visual aids.) The speaker carried on like the pro she is.

There's a Fire in the Building. You are responsible for your audience. Did you ever think of that? You're the person standing up front, the one with the microphone. All attention is on you. Should an emergency, such as a fire, occur, you're the person the audience will look to for guidance.

You must keep a cool head and react quickly. Don't announce the nature of the emergency. Saying that there is a fire in the building could cause panic and worsen the situation.

People seldom take notice of fire exits; you must point them out. Announce at the beginning of your program where the emergency exits are, and call attention to the fastest route exiting the building. You may be speaking to a group who has never been in that building before. They need to know where the exits are before, not after, an emergency occurs.

Someone in the Audience Gets Sick. Should someone become ill during your speech they might slip quietly out of the room. Then again they may not be able to. You may not notice someone ill at first, but those sitting around the person will, and there's sure to be a commotion. First, stop talking, because no one will be interested in anything you have to say. Then take control of the situation. If you're on a microphone ask if there is a doctor in the room. If the situation warrants, don't hesitate to have someone dial 911. I heard a story about a speaker who had a person die in his audience. When it became apparent the person was dead, the speaker led the audience in prayer.

That's Not How You Rehearsed It. No matter how much time you spend rehearsing your speech, it could happen that what you wanted to say and what comes out of your mouth are two different things. No big deal. If it's just a matter of the wrong word, simply repeat the sentence with the correct word.

Tripping over your tongue is another common problem. I remember once having difficulty saying "extemporaneously." It's a word I use all the time in my workshops, but one day I just couldn't get the word out of my mouth. I tried several times; each attempt got worse. I must have sounded like Porky Pig.

Don't draw attention to the fact that you flubbed a word or made a slip of the tongue; the audience will know. Don't make the mistake worse by saying "Excuse me" or "whoops."

If you say something that ends up not making sense because you said the words out of order, back up and simply say, "Let me try that again," then repeat the phrase. There's no need to make a remark about your false teeth. The less said about the flub the better.

You Forgot What You Were Going to Say! The audience has never heard your speech. They won't know that you left something out unless you tell them. Don't make a big deal about forgetting a part of your speech.

When I forget part of a speech, I say, "There's something else I want to tell you. . . ." Saying this allows me not only to get in the information I forgot, but the audience thinks I'm giving them something extra. This is much better than saying, "Oh, I forgot to tell you. . . ."

You Can't Remember a Particular Word. Turn this problem into an advantage. Ask the audience for their help in getting the word right. I was right in the middle of illustrating a main point when I forgot that thing mechanics use to loosen large pipes. I asked the audience, "What's that thing called?" I quickly got responses from several people who beamed with pride for having the correct answer.

You Get a Case of the Clumsies. Tripping onto the stage is not what you planned, nor was bumping into the table and spilling a glass of water, but you did. So, big deal. Yes, these things are embarrassing and have happened to hundreds of speakers at one time or another. I have always found that humor relieves tension and works wonders when things go wrong. Your audience doesn't want to be placed in an embarrassing situation any more than you. So, you tripped. Pretend to pick up a stone and toss it aside and say, "There, now, no one else will trip."

If you drop a pencil or something falls off the lectern, leave it. Don't draw attention to it by bending to pick it up.

You Lost Your Place. I love what Nanette Fabray did while speaking to a packed house. Nanette has a casual, folksy speaking style and talks directly to her audience. She has a tendency to ramble and lose her place, which is no problem for her. When she realized she had lost her place, she simply asked the people in the front row, "Can somebody tell me where I was?" Everyone laughed and sure enough someone in the front row knew where she had left off and got her back on track. There was no frustration on her part. She made light of it and even announced at the beginning of her presentation that she often wandered off her subject. Nanette could get away with this because she is a comedian and comedians do funny things. We expected her to do something witty and funny, and she didn't disappoint us. You might try the same approach, situation permitting.

It Wasn't Supposed to Rain Today. Your umbrella, raincoat, and boots are neatly tucked away in the hall closet. You have a fifty dollar hairdo, and while on the way to your speaking engagement it begins to rain. If you walk from your car to the building, you're going to look like one of those drenched cats in a cartoon. Make sure you have your umbrella, rain bonnet, and rain boots handy. Never leave home without them.

Things That Fly in Your Face. Speaking outdoors can turn into a plot straight from a Stephen King novel. Thankfully it doesn't happen often, but when it does, it's annoying, a distrac-

tion for both you and the audience, not to mention embarrassing. I'm talking about those pesky flying insects. Flies, gnats, and
bees buzz around you as if you're the main course at a Sunday
picnic. You can swat at them all you want, but they aren't about
to leave. You could have fun with the situation by saying, "Did
he pay to get in?" or you could pretend to hold a can of insect
repellent and spray the pest in mid-air. You'll get a good laugh.

If you know you'll be speaking outdoors, don't wear perfume
or body powder that attracts insects, and use a nonscented hair
spray.

You Suddenly Have to Go to the Restroom.   Nerves can
cause the urgent need to go to the restroom. Don't wait until
you're being introduced to decide you have to go. Planning,
planning, planning, remember? Find out if there will be a break
between the meal and your talk. If not, and you just can't wait,
quietly slip out during dinner and take care of business.

The Building Loses Electricity.   The lights just went out in
the middle of your presentation. Most often the lights will come
back on within a few seconds, but if they don't, take control
and draw upon your reserve humor and say, "I guess I'm finished." Keep in mind there may be people who are afraid of the
dark. Before the audience tries to escape the darkened room,
ask everyone to stay in their seats and lead them in song. Good
voice or not, the audience will be grateful for something to do
and will enjoy the interruption.

Your Microphone Dies.   Doc Blakely, Ph.D., professional
speaker and humorist, says, "There are only three kinds of speakers: Those who have experienced microphone failure, those who
will experience microphone failure, and those who will experience microphone failure again."

Keeping that in mind, the odds are that if you speak in public long enough, sooner or later (we all hope later), and even
though you checked the microphone thoroughly, you will have
a microphone suddenly die in the middle of your speech. The
big question is, what will you do when it's your turn?

Your choices are to faint, stand there mouthing inaudible
sounds in hopes your audience can lip read, tap dance, or go

into a Marcel Marceau act and pantomime the poor soul locked in a glass box. Or you could increase your volume and continue without the microphone. Handle the situation with humor. A remark, no matter how corny, will relieve the tension.

Advise the technicians of the problem and let them handle it. Use the interruption to your advantage. Walk out among the audience, shake hands and talk to individuals. Use the time to pass out handouts, or motion for everyone to stand and stretch.

The Audience Is Smaller Than You Expected. A low point for any speaker is to have fewer people than expected show up for your presentation. It's deflating, but it happens frequently, especially at service clubs where membership attendance varies. Don't take the low attendance personally. People are busy and a hundred other things scream for their time. You must go on and do your best for the small but appreciative audience, and never show disappointment.

You're Too Short for the Lectern. Few women stand six feet tall. The average woman's height is five foot six inches (sixty-six inches). The average height of the standard lectern stands four feet or forty-eight inches. Boiled down to inches, this means that someone like myself, who stands five foot five inches, has only eighteen inches of her body seen above the lectern. That's not much if you want to use gestures effectively. You can do two things to compensate for munchkins at the lectern. One, get away from the lectern all together, and second, place a block behind the lectern to stand on. Make sure the block is large enough for you to move your feet at least twelve inches apart. I've seen telephone books used as a last-minute height saver. Please don't do this. I watched in amusement as a speaker slowly slid off a stack of telephone books.

There Is No Lectern! You asked for a lectern, but when you arrived there wasn't one. If you have a lot of notes written on large sheets of paper, this is going to be a problem. Use a table, if available, for supporting your notes. Otherwise, stand with your feet flat on the floor, slightly apart for good balance. Hold your notes in one hand and use the other for gesturing. Sure the notes will be a distraction, but with a dynamic delivery, the audience will be so involved in what you're saying they'll soon forget about them unless you wave them around.

You're Too Ill to Speak. Most professional speakers I have talked with say that no matter how ill they are, they find reserve strength to do the job expected of them. As professional speakers, they know the importance of showing up and doing the very best job they can. They can fall apart afterward.

Even though you may not be a professional speaker, accepting the opportunity of speaking carries with it a huge responsibility. People are depending on you to show up and speak. If you become ill several days before your scheduled speech, you have time to call your contact person and let her know, giving her time to find a replacement. But what if you suddenly become ill hours prior to the speech? Before you call your contact person, try to find someone to cover for you who is familiar with your topic and knows how to deliver a great performance. It's better than leaving a program coordinator in a bind. If you can't find someone to replace you, the last resort is to cancel. Maybe that should be another part of your planning process. Think about who could replace you should you become too ill to speak.

You Have a Head Cold, Your Throat Hurts, Your Nose Is All Stuffed Up, and You Sound Like a Toad. Having a head cold, sinus problems, or sore throat causes the voice to sound raspy and nasal. These conditions can spring upon you overnight, and often do. They aren't serious enough to cancel your speech, but the sound of your voice may not be clear or pleasant sounding. Audiences are forgiving. They'll feel special knowing that despite your head cold (unless you sneeze on them) or sinus problems you made the effort to come and speak to them. It's important that you explain up front that your voice doesn't always sound this way. Tell them you have a head cold and that you aren't contagious. Ask them to bear with you. If you don't explain the reason for the raspiness or hoarseness, the audience will be distracted, wondering what's wrong with you. Does she always sound like that? By explaining up front, everyone can concentrate on your message not your voice. Don't apologize for your condition, just explain it.

Laryngitis Strikes. Laryngitis is a problem that can't be overlooked. When laryngitis occurs, the best thing you can do is give your voice a rest. Doctors will tell you to save your voice. Don't add to the strain and worsen the condition by talking. Good advice. Take it.

Oh, No, Diarrhea and Vomiting! Nerves can do crazy things to our bodies. If you're prone to diarrhea or vomiting, don't eat before you speak. Ask your pharmacist to suggest an antidiarrhea medication; unfortunately, there is little in the way of medication that will prevent vomiting. Be prepared. Check the route to the nearest restroom. Should you become ill during your speech, the only thing you can do is leave the platform, run to the restroom, and throw up.

Headache, Sour Stomach, and Dry Mouth. There are many over-the-counter medications such as aspirin, antacid, and lemon candy that work for all of these problems. A migraine headache can range from a mild nuisance to a throbbing, demobilizing pain and may take a prescription drug to diminish its agony.

There are many things that can go wrong while making a speech, and it's inevitable, if you speak often, someday something will go wrong. Supreme Court Justice Sandra Day O'Connor says when making a decision in a case, she puts all her time and effort at the front end of trying to decide correctly. "Then I don't agonize over it. I may have to live with the consequences, but I'm going to live with them without regrets. I did the best I could at the time," she said.

Justice O'Connor's beliefs can also be applied to making a speech. You can only do your best. If something happens that ruins your presentation and is no fault of your own, the healthy thing to do is move on. Don't let the mistake or problem live with you. Forget about it. I can assure you that ninety-nine percent of your audience forgot about whatever went wrong two minutes after leaving the room.

Handling Those Very Personal Female Problems

PMS. It's been called the "Curse." Some say it has to do with Eve and the apple. Women don't give a damn who or what caused it, all we know is that for a few days just before our menstrual cycle we feel like a big pile of dog poop dropped into a blender and served up on a bed of hot nails. We suffer from irritability, depression, and mood swings. We lose our temper and endure physical discomforts such as headaches, bloating, cramps, nervousness, breast swelling and tenderness, weight gain, and acne. And that's just the first day. We want to yell, "I'm suffering from PMS, you don't want to piss me off."

There are many things you can do to ward off or minimize the symptoms of PMS. If you have a regular menstrual cycle, chart your cycle and mark on your calendar or in a daily diary the day that you begin flowing. If you're asked to speak during those times and know it's a time of living hell, you can decline gracefully with no explanation necessary.

Doctors suggest eating foods high in potassium such as bananas, tomatoes, and whole-grain breads. Vitamin supplements can help. Avoid alcohol and reduce the amount of salt and caffeine (that includes chocolate, sorry) the week before your period. If you don't already have a regular exercise routine, begin one now, not only for the benefits you receive during menstruation, but to feel better and have more energy during your speech.

There are many over-the-counter medicines designed to relieve bloating and reduce the effects of PMS, but consult your doctor before using them.

Hot Flashes. Women beginning the journey into menopause may experience many strange and uncomfortable symptoms associated with this rite of passage. One such problem is hot flashes. While some hot flashes may be mild and occur occasionally, others may be severe, uncomfortable, and embarrassing, rendering you ineffective for their duration.

Other conditions resulting from menopause are emotional, such as depression and irritability. You're already nervous about speaking before a group of strangers, you don't need the additional emotional tension.

Estrogen replacement therapy is one way to alleviate these problems. The elimination of hot flashes, control of emotional symptoms, and reduction of bone loss through osteoporosis are both the short- and long-term benefits of estrogen therapy. Only your doctor can prescribe the method (creams, oral tablets, injection, or patches) and dosage that will work best for you. How do I know these things? Been there. Did that.

Excessive Perspiration. There are many antiperspirants on the market today and by now you have found the one that works best for you. However, when under stress, your regular antiperspirant may fail. Wearing dress shields helps. They're simple to use and protect your clothing, saving you the embarrassment of underarm wetness.

There are several products on the market for excessive facial perspiration. Check with your cosmetic consultant for advice on which works best.

With all the many things that can go wrong while making a speech, it's a wonder anyone would want to place themselves in such a situation, but millions do. They make speeches because they know they have something important to share and that others will benefit by what they say. They also know that no problem is so big or worrisome that it can't be solved. The trick, as with all phases of public speaking, is in the planning. Plan for those things that could go wrong.

11

The Communication Process

I know you believe you understand what you think I said, but I am not sure you realize that what you heard is not really what I meant.

Author unknown

No public speaking book is complete without a chapter on the communication process. It's important to understand what role the audience plays so you can tell how effective you are in reaching them and to recognize the distractions they may be experiencing.

Public speaking is a two-way process. The sender (speaker) transmits a verbal or nonverbal message that is decoded by the receiver. The receiver (audience) sends feedback to the speaker, who then interprets the feedback and, if necessary, sends out another message. This process continues until each party has the necessary information needed for understanding.

That's basic Communications 101, but I'm frequently surprised how many speakers don't have a clue why they aren't connecting with their audience.

THE FOUR P'S OF AUDIENCE DISTRACTION

Put yourself in the place of your audience for a moment. As a member of the audience at a seminar, board meeting, or sales presentation have you ever found yourself distracted by people talking, car horns blowing outside, or a speaker's mannerism? Have you ever been too cold or too hot, uncomfortable because of ill-fitting clothes, or had something on your mind other than the speaker?

Distractions bombarded you. They challenge your concentration and draw your attention away from the speaker, making it difficult to give her your undivided attention. And even if these disturbances are for only an instant, it takes an effort to pull your attention back to the speaker and her message.

From a speaker's point of view, distractions are annoying when you realize that your audience most likely has missed something you've said.

Distractions can easily be overcome if you recognize their cause and learn what to do about them. It's important that you learn to recognize the different types of distractions your audience might face.

There are four types of distractions. I call them the terrible P's: Physical, Psychological, Prejudicial, and Personal.

Physical Distractions

Physical distractions come in many forms; some are:

• Noise. Inside noises are usually people coughing or sneezing, someone dropping a book, the scraping of a chair on the floor, talking, the clatter of dishes being dropped, or the fan motor on an air conditioner. Outside noise may be an airplane flying overhead, the wail of an emergency vehicle, the voice of another speaker or applause coming from a concurrent breakout session next door, or the music from the lounge down the hall.

• Room temperature. Preset thermostats can cause a room to be too cool or too warm. A temperature that was comfortable for the last group that met in that room may not be satisfactory for your group. Also, keep in mind, a room that is comfortable while empty is likely to become too warm when filled.

• Late arrivals. For some reason, when the door opens every head in the audience turns to see who's coming in. I don't know why; that's just the way it is.

• Up-stagers. Those are things in view of the audience but not the speaker. I have sat watching a bug crawl up the pant leg of a speaker, people walk behind the curtain, a window shade cord swing in the breeze. Thank goodness all these things didn't happen to the same speaker.

• Pagers. What would the world be like without our electronic umbilical cord? You can bet if there's a doctor in your audience, he or she will be beeped and have to leave. Most doctors know from experience to sit in the back of the room for this reason. But when they don't or can't, their departure will be a distraction. But at least pagers have a silent signal. I've sat in audiences where cellular phones rang and businessmen sat with laptop computers on the table. Talk about distractions.

• Talkers. There is no other description for them but rude. Yet there will always be those who just have to talk no matter what the situation. When someone else talks while you're trying to speak, it means you've lost the ears of two people—the talker and the one being talked to. And there is a good chance those around the talker are also being distracted.

• Sound system. Nothing can jar the nerves more than the squeal of high-pitched feedback from an improperly adjusted microphone.

• Poor lighting. Dim overhead lights make note taking difficult. Poorly adjusted lights can glare on the viewing screen. Sometimes a light attached to the lectern reflects into the front row of seats. An unfocused spotlight can leave you standing in semi-darkness or shine in the audience's eyes.

I arrived late for a presentation. (No, I wasn't the speaker.) As I entered the auditorium, I heard a voice coming from the corner of the stage but saw no speaker. I looked harder. I saw only a tiny glare from the speaker's eyeglasses suspended in the darkness. Apparently she had been showing slides. The lights had been dimmed but not turned up again after the slide show. That can happen when you are engrossed in what you're doing. Think through your presentation, not only for the speech itself, but for details such as what's happening to the lights.

• Poor acoustics. Some rooms such as gymnasiums and church social halls were never meant to be used for making a speech. They're large and hollow, causing the voice to echo.

• Clothing. After a meal, girdles get tighter, belts shrink, and for some unknown reason shoes suddenly don't fit. If you are speaking after a meal, there's a good chance the audience will be uncomfortable and not as attentive.

• The room itself can be a distraction. I attended a business-women's meeting where the audience faced four large windows. Late in the afternoon the sun shone into our eyes, the speaker was in silhouette, and every car that went by became an added distraction. I have never figured out why someone hasn't arranged the chairs to face the other direction. The layout of the room, physical obstructions, and seating arrangements are just a few of the many ways a room can cause distractions.

Psychological Distractions

People come to your presentation with personal baggage filled with problems ranging from troubles with a spouse, child, or boss, to health and financial woes. They bring their troubles and flop them down in front of you. You can't resolve their problems, but if your speech is interesting, you can get them to forget them for a time. But always bear in mind, people will be distracted by what is going on in their lives, whether it's good or bad, and you may never get them totally involved in your presentation.

Personal Distractions

The time of day. As I said in chapter 2, the time of day affects people differently. There are early morning people who jump out of bed at 5 A.M. raring to go, and the night owls who can't get their eyes open before noon. Others come alive after 5 P.M. Take into consideration the time of day and how it affects your audience.

If you're speaking before lunch, the audience may be hungry and distracted by the grumbling in their stomachs. If your audience has just eaten a big meal, chances are some people will grow sleepy and nod off.

Sometimes a member of your audience will take a mental journey, fantasize, or reminisce. Others may daydream and meditate, while the rest may be planning what to have for dinner. Even the excitement of going on a two-week cruise to the Bahamas could cause a distraction. Your challenge is to be so dynamic that you draw the audience back from their mental journeys.

You can be the cause of the distraction, too, by something you say. Ever hear a word or phrase that triggered a thought of something that happened long ago? Before you realize it, you've drifted off into dreamland and didn't hear a word the speaker said. That can happen to your audience, also, and the real problem is that you won't know when it happens until you see the glazed look in their eyes. That's why it is so important to maintain constant eye contact with your audience.

This might sound strange, but for me as a member of an audience, I am distracted by the placement of the U.S. flag. It's a personal thing with me and maybe you have no concerns one way or the other, but being a veteran, I have deep regard and respect for our flag and like to see it displayed correctly. If you're a politician, with cameras focused on you, I strongly suggest you make sure the flag is on the correct side of the lectern—behind and to your right as you face the audience.

Prejudicial Distractions

This type of distraction is one I wish I didn't have to talk about, but it's real and must be mentioned. There will always be those who don't like what you look or sound like because of your nationality, race, or because you are a woman. Maybe you have a physical disability or slight speech impediment. Some audience members prejudge you because of your voice, what you're wearing, your hairstyle, accent, or just because the subject is not one the listener wants to hear.

HANDLING DISTRACTIONS

Deal with distractions immediately. Get the problem(s) out of the way, so you can move on. Learning to recognize the terrible P's is one thing, knowing how to deal with them is another. Let's look at some ways to best handle distractions.

Outside noise, such as the scream of an emergency vehicle or the roar of an airplane, can't easily be ignored. It's best to pause and hold up one finger in a wait-a-minute gesture. The audience will understand. Wait for the noise to subside, then proceed by repeating the last thing you said. Your audience will appreciate that you stopped so they didn't miss anything.

If there is a disturbance in the room, should you acknowledge it or ignore it? It depends on the situation. Say a waiter drops a tray of dishes. You know everyone in the room heard the dishes hit the floor and are probably embarrassed for the waiter. Keep the situation light by making a casual remark. A funny remark will break the tension, allowing time for everyone to deal with the disturbance.

Once when a telephone persistently rang in the next room I said, "Somebody please answer that. If that's the White House, tell them I'm busy."

What you can do will depend on the type of noise. If the noise is a jackhammer, it isn't going to go away anytime soon. Raise your volume and press on. If it's impossible for anyone to hear, you may need to take drastic action and move to another location.

If a noise in the hall continues, ask someone to close the door. That's seems simple enough, but I am surprised how many speakers will continue, competing with the noise. If the noise comes from the session in the next room, I usually say something like, "Must have been a drill instructor" or "He would have no difficulty being heard in Yankee Stadium." Raise your voice a notch higher and continue. Your microphone should help you. Of course, the guy next door has to raise his voice to talk over you, and now you have dueling speakers.

The audience will wait for you to make the first move to handle the distraction. How you handle it will set a mood and attitude for the audience. If you seem annoyed by the disturbance, it will leave the audience feeling that your attention has been divided between the disturbance and them. Always let your audience know they're number one.

Room temperature can be handled by checking the thermostat before you start. If you notice someone fanning herself or looking as though she's uncomfortable, tell the audience to bear with you, you know it's warm, but you'll be through in two (five) minutes. If you still have an hour to go, stop, find the thermostat, or have a maintenance person set the temperature you desire. Open windows, if possible, and give the audience a second to take off their coats. Do something, anything, to make the audience more comfortable. Remember, your audience will probably feel the room's temperature before you do. I get so involved in my presentation that I seldom notice if it is freezing. I must constantly rely on feedback from the audience to know what's going on.

You can do two things with latecomers. First, if the person slips in quietly in the back of the room and few people notice, ignore the intrusion and continue talking. Never look at the person coming in; that only causes others to look to see what you're looking at. Your second choice is to acknowledge the person. Stop talking and wait until they're seated, then continue with your program. Depending on the situation, you can welcome the latecomer and help her find a seat. Otherwise the person could become an even greater disruption while trying to find an empty chair.

Sometimes someone will come in to deliver a message. If the person they need is seated in the rear, there won't be much disruption. But if they are in the front, you can bet everyone's attention will be on the messenger. Again, pause until the person has delivered the message, then continue.

The solution to a disturbing sound system and lighting problems is to check them before the audience arrives. Test the volume on the sound system and turn the lights to the level you will be using during your presentation, and check to see if any light shines into the audience area.

If no break has been offered between the meal and your presentation, make one. Build a stand-and-stretch into your speech.

Allow everyone a chance to use the facilities, loosen clothing, or whatever they need to be comfortable.

Techniques for handling psychological and personal distraction include: pulling the audience back into your speech by increasing your volume, making a grand gesture or body movement, walking among the audience, and calling for a stand-and-stretch minute. If possible, refer to people by name, such as, "Isn't that so, John?" or "Don't you think so, Mary?" Don't ever embarrass someone because they drifted off, just pull them gently back into your speech.

Unfortunately, there is little you can do about prejudicial distractions. If the audience doesn't like you because you're a woman, it's not your problem. Realize that their prejudices are *their* problem, they're the ones who have to deal with it. Ignore the folded arms and scowling faces. Smile and be the best you know how to be. They're the ones missing a wonderful or important message because of their closed minds.

Almost all distractions can be overcome if handled properly. Knowing what to do when distractions occur increases your effectiveness, and showing that you are aware of the distraction says you're on top of things and in control.

UNDERSTANDING NONVERBAL FEEDBACK

Never assume that just because your audience is looking at you they are interested or listening. Open eyes don't necessarily mean open ears. Audience feedback is the only yardstick that tells you if your audience understands your message or is paying attention. It's important, therefore, to recognize nonverbal feedback signals, both positive and negative.

Positive signals, such as smiles, note taking, and nodding heads are wonderful and need no improvement, but negative feedback requires immediate adjustments. Furrowed brows and questioning looks may mean a person doesn't understand. Restlessness, staring out the window, or yawns are signs of boredom. Scowling, rigid body posture, eyes rolled toward the ceiling with arms folded across the chest could mean disagreement or disinterest.

Not all scowls and furrowed brows are negative signals. I have watched members of audiences as they listened to other speakers. I believe their scowls and furrowed brows were due to intense concentration, because they laughed in all the right places and responded to the speaker in other positive ways. Don't be misled by some people's expressions.

Once after a very long week of conference meetings, the last meeting of the day was more than my body could handle. I found myself dozing off. It wasn't the speaker's fault. An atom bomb couldn't have kept me awake. If you notice someone in your audience with his head bent as if in prayer or with his head resting on his notebook, sound asleep, don't wake him. The guy probably needs the rest. Above all, don't blame yourself for being ineffective. His slumber may not be your fault.

If only one or two people in an audience of fifty are shifting in their seats, don't worry; it could be they have gas. If more than half are squirming around, though, it's a sign of a problem that you must address immediately. Stop talking and ask what the problem is.

The main thing is always to keep an eye on your audience and watch for feedback. Become sensitive to their needs. Put yourself in their place.

12

Humor—No Laughing Matter

*Cleaning your house while your kids are still growing
is like shoveling the walk before it stops snowing.*

PHYLLIS DILLER, *Housekeeping Hints*

Your talk should not only inform, inspire, or persuade, but should be entertaining as well. When an audience is having fun, they'll remember what you say longer, and if you tell a funny story, there's a good chance of that story being retold in the office the next day, giving your message a second audience. Days, even weeks, following a speech, the audience may not remember your name or the main point of your topic, but they'll remember that you made them laugh and forget their worries for a few minutes.

THE POWER OF HUMOR

Humor is a powerful tool. It takes a magnifying glass to the human condition and makes us see life from a new perspective. It makes us stop and look at ourselves in our underwear while standing on a busy street corner. Humor bridges prejudices and preconceptions, helps people learn as it persuades and sells. It acts as a safety net that keeps us from falling on our face. Using humor implies you are confident and in control.

If we can laugh when the world is falling apart around us, we will survive. With all that humor does, can you afford not using it in your speech whenever possible?

Mark Twain said, "The human race has only one effective weapon and that is laughter." Dr. Ralph C. Smedley, founder of Toastmasters International, said, "We learn best in moments of enjoyment."

But what is humor, and how can you accomplish it in your speech? First, what humor *isn't*. It's not a string of jokes or one-liners with a punch line delivered like a stand-up comic in an effort to keep the audience in a constant state of laughter.

Humor is sneaking up on the audience, tickling them with a story, then standing back and watching the fun you caused. You don't have to tell a joke to be funny. Humor can be saying something that makes the audience laugh or giggle, or humor can be a gesture or expression that gives special meaning to words that otherwise would sound ordinary.

WHERE DO YOU FIND FUNNY STORIES?

You say you aren't funny? You probably are and just don't know it. Do you see humor in everyday situations? Do you laugh when others say funny things? Do you see a brighter side to a serious situation? Do you see funny uses for common objects? And can you laugh at yourself? A "yes" answer to any of these questions is a sign that you have the instincts for seeing the funnier side of life.

The instant you see something funny, write it down. Don't rely on memory. More good jokes and stories have been lost because they couldn't be remembered a few hours later.

Funny signs, posters, bumper stickers, and billboards that make you laugh will make others laugh, too. Watch for funny things about people, places, and events. TV commercials are another good source for humor. As you gather bits and pieces,

group them into categories. You may not be able to use everything, but someday one of those funny things you saw or heard
will fit into your talk.

Another place to find material for humor is the library. There
you'll find joke books—most are alphabetized by subject. Scan
newspapers and magazines for funny stories.

TECHNIQUES FOR TICKLING THE FUNNY BONE

1. *Use firsthand stories.* Keep on constant lookout for funny
situations that occur at work, home, while shopping, in church,
and while traveling. And never overlook the funny things kids
say and do.

2. *Personalize your stories.* The more believable you can make
a story, the more intrigued the audience will become with the
tale. Go though your collected stories and place yourself in them.
Substitute your name for the character's, change the pronouns to
I or me, and tell the story as you or a close friend observed it.

3. *Take advantage of a spontaneous situation or remark.* In an
informal speaking situation you have leeway to play off comments from the audience.

4. *Use quips and asides.* In the middle of your speech you
mention the word *chaperone*, pause, and say, "You know what
a chaperone is, don't you? A form of fire extinguisher."

5. *Use vocal exaggeration.* "Well, excuuuuuuuuse me," became
a popular gag line several years ago.

6. *Exaggerate or overstate an everyday situation.* "I don't want
to say that her house was dirty, but there were things growing
in her refrigerator that had begun to teach their young."

7. *Build on a series of three.* This technique works well
because the story you tell has a triple whammy. Just when the
audience thinks you have told the joke, you say something else
that builds on the first comment. Then after the laughter has
died down you throw out the zinger of the third line.

8. *Poke fun at yourself.* Telling on yourself makes you real
and gives the audience something they can identify with. They
have been in embarrassing situations too, and it feels good not

to be out there alone. A word of caution: Be careful when poking fun at yourself. Avoid comments that devalue you as a woman or make you appear to have little self-worth.

9. *Poke fun at authority.* In describing a politician's lengthy speech, a speaker said, "His speeches are a spectacle for the eyes, a revelation to the ears, and a challenge for the kidneys." Politics is the art of looking for trouble, finding it everywhere, diagnosing it incorrectly, and applying the wrong remedies.

10. *Make light of a serious situation.* I won a humorous speech contest once with a story about how I got to Europe. The event wasn't funny at the time, and only after a ten-year distance could I stand back and see the humor in the situation. I gave the speech titled "One Small Problem" and had a good time poking fun at myself and the situation I had gotten into because I was terrified of flying.

11. *Twist the meaning.* A friend of mine told the story about how she locked herself out of her house while taking out the garbage in her underwear. She gave a new meaning to "neighborhood watch."

12. *Paint a funny picture.* In my story about going to Europe, I tell about my fear of flying and how, when on the plane, I took hold of my husband's knee on my right and a stranger's knee on my left and began Lamaze. Taking short breaths, I single-handedly got the plane off the ground.

13. *Describe an absurd or outrageous situation.* How about forming a Foster Parent Plant Program (FPPP), a governmental agency, which oversees and investigates the foster parents program, inspects homes, and sets up a monitoring system for abused plants?

14. *A planned malapropism.* Use a wrong but similar-sounding word. For example, "I don't eat meat because I'm a veterinarian." "The best remedy for constipation is milk of amnesia." "The Bible forbade fortification," or "I like to go on the cannibal rides."

15. *The pun.* Some say the pun is the lowest form of humor. Oscar Levant said, "A pun is the lowest form of humor when you didn't think of it first." It's all in the perception. I like puns. For me, puns are funny, and the cleverness of a pun always

intrigues me. A pun may not always solicit a belly laugh from your audience—a moan would be more likely—but try it anyway. "The dead skunk in the middle of the road story may be funny on the surface, but . . ."

SUGGESTIONS FOR USING HUMOR

1. *Tell only stories that make you laugh.* You must first believe in the story before asking the audience to believe it's funny.

2. *The story must have a point that supports your purpose.* If the story doesn't propel your speech forward, leave it out.

3. *Keep the story short.* Long explanations or lengthy descriptions destroy the story's effect.

4. *The story must fit the audience and the occasion.* Find a joke about the group you're addressing, i.e., military wives, secretaries, doctors, lawyers, volunteers, et cetera, then personalize it for the group. This is one time you better know your audience. Humor is a delicate creature and not every story or joke will get the same response from all audiences. Know if your remarks might offend. Be sure your audience will understand the point of the joke. All the questions you asked in chapter 2 about knowing your audience should be asked again when inserting humor into your speech.

5. *Stories must be timely.* Just as all your facts, statistics, and information must be current, your humor should also be fresh. That doesn't mean you can't tell an old joke. Some topics and jokes never die. Others fade fast. When George Bush said, "Read my lips," every comedian in the country picked up on it and the line was funny for a long time. Use that line now and you're likely to get a groan.

6. *Don't use regional humor.* Jokes about things that happen in a specific area of the country will be understood and appreciated by those living there, but the humor may be lost to others outside of the region. Even humor from city to city may have limits. (Pun intended.)

7. *Pause.* Take your time before delivering the punch line. Everything is in the timing when telling a funny story or joke.

A well-placed pause just before delivering the punch line adds tension and impact. The tension causes the audience to listen more intently. It says to the audience, "Here comes the funny stuff, get ready to laugh."

8. *Wait for the laughter.* Don't stifle the audience by jumping the laugh. Tell the story at a conversational rate of speech, hit the punch line, pause, and give the audience time to digest the story, then wait for the laugh. Don't talk over the laughter; bask in its glory. Inexperienced speakers tend to rush on when they don't immediately hear laughter. Build in time for applause. That wonderful sound! And should spontaneous applause or laughter erupt during the speech, pause until it has subsided before continuing.

9. *Find your own style.* Is it deadpan, self-mocking, dry, or cynical? Your level of comfort using humor will determine your style. This will come through experience.

10. *Memorize the punch line.* Humor, whether a story or a joke, must be spontaneous, and fails miserably when read. Practice telling your story or joke until you know it backward and forward. Larry Wilde, author of many books on humor writes, ". . . no matter how poorly you relate the initial parts of the joke, you will have the security of knowing you can deliver the punch line correctly."

WHAT'S NOT FUNNY

1. *Off-color and offensive jokes that are racist or sexist are* always *in bad taste.*

2. *Vulgarity.* I can't think of one instance where profanity is welcome or appropriate. And nothing is a bigger turn-off than to hear a woman use foul language, even if repeating a story told by someone else.

3. *Jokes that insult or ridicule an individual.* You aren't Don Rickles, and unless you are speaking at a roast, don't even think about doing the insult or ridicule routine. Don Rickles can get away with cutting remarks, but you'll look small in the eyes of the audience and lose their respect, and I can guarantee you won't be asked to speak to that group again.

4. *Pot shots at religious, racial, and ethnic groups.* More and more people are becoming sensitive about their background, and you never know who you may offend. You might get away with poking fun at a group you belong to because you're poking fun at yourself, too, but as an outsider it becomes harmful, making you appear as if you think you're superior.

5. *Pot shots at animals.* Stories about shooting Bambi don't go over well with animal lovers. Dead cat stories were popular a few years ago. I remember the groans they got. They'll fall flat today for sure.

6. *Making fun of a strongly held belief.* Many people believe in UFOs. Some claim to have been taken aboard and physically examined. This may sound absurd to many people, but to those experiencing the abduction it's no joke. Be careful when you tread on someone's beliefs.

7. *Insider jokes.* Jokes or comments directed to only a few in the loop make others feel left out.

8. *Sarcastic comments about someone's appearance.* People come in all shapes and sizes. That's the way we were made. Make fun of someone's height or weight and you not only hurt feelings, you will find yourself answering to lawyers. People are sensitive these days.

9. *Seriously painful situations or subjects.* Highway accidents caused by drunk drivers, children with terminal diseases, or the elderly with Alzheimer's disease are not funny.

Humor Squelchers

• Telegraphing. Don't announce that you are about to say something funny. "I'm going to tell you a joke" or "Now, here's a funny story" will fail every time because the audience will challenge you to make them laugh. The object is to move into your story and let the humor of it creep up and surprise your listeners.

• Explaining your joke. If they didn't "get it," move on.

• Laughing at your own joke before the punch line is delivered.

• Apologizing if the humor or joke doesn't work.

WHAT TO DO WHEN YOU LAY AN EGG

If your story or joke falls flat, don't panic, and don't blame the audience for not getting the point. When you lay an egg, make an omelet. Take advantage of the silence by playing on the fact that the joke didn't work. While holding notes up to the light or adjusting glasses, say, "Says here, 'Pause for laughter.'" By making light of the situation you defuse the embarrassment the audience feels for not laughing even though they knew they should have.

Humorist Doc Blakely says that if they don't get the joke or laugh, pretend you're serious.

I once heard a speaker say that he never told a funny story unless he felt sure the majority of the audience had heard it before. He said familiar stories are best because people like proving their own sophistication knowing the latest joke. They feel more comfortable knowing just when to burst out laughing.

Judith C. Tingley says, "The increased use of humor in general and the careful use of 'put-down humor' helps you look confident and in charge." Note that she says "careful use" of humor.

Sir Alan Patrick Herbert, English statesman, once said, "There is no reason why a joke should not be appreciated more than once. Imagine how little good music there would be if, for example, a conductor refused to play Beethoven's Fifth Symphony on the ground that his audience might have heard it before." And George Jessel said, "Don't be afraid of an old joke. A really good joke, like a melody, lives eternally."

Recycled jokes are fine, but they must be relevant to your subject. Give the joke a new twist or personalize it. Mold the story to fit your speaking style. Using humor, especially when you relate it to yourself, makes you more human and vulnerable and endears you to the audience.

PART III

Speaking Situations

13

The Executive Briefing

*If you're going to play the game properly
you'd better know every rule.*

BARBARA JORDAN, *Barbara Jordan*

The executive briefing is different from other types of speaking situations, and is defined as the preparation and presentation of critical information for the purpose of explaining, instructing, persuading, or reporting. As a manager, you may be required to relate information on a status or financial report, or explain a reduction in work force, or report on an employee problem. Executive briefings are a challenge that can advance your career.

The executive briefing has specific requirements, characteristics, and guidelines that must be followed. You will be presenting information to the decision makers of large companies. To reach these executives, you must understand how they think and what they want and expect from a briefing presenter.

As with any other speech, you will still need to address the twenty-six questions of preparation (chapter 2) with special attention given to the purpose of your speech. Know who will be in the audience and their position with the company. Find out how much they already know about your subject. This cuts down on the amount of background information you need to give.

SEVENTEEN CRITICAL QUESTIONS

Executives look at the overall picture. Their primary concern is the long-term financial stability of their entire company or organization. The information you present must focus on the bottom-line benefits for the company.

According to Raymond A. Slesinski, president of Genesis Training Solutions, when you present a briefing to executives, you must answer the following questions:

• What exactly is the problem and why is it important? How does the problem affect the overall health of the company? What potential short- and long-term impact does the problem have on the company? What has already been done about the problem? What may happen if nothing is done?

• What are the specific tangible and intangible benefits of your proposal? What are the perceived drawbacks, problems, limitations, special requirements, and risks associated with it? How can these things best be handled? Why is this particular program/design recommended over other options available?

• When can the solution be implemented? How long will it take? What resources and actions are needed to implement it? What benchmarks can be used as a measure for the progress and success of the proposal?

• How much will it cost? What short- and long-term returns can be expected? How can you prove the project or proposal will produce the desired overall technical, operational, and financial outcomes? Why should the proposal be implemented immediately?

By looking at this list of questions, you can see the executive briefing isn't for the unprepared, disorganized, or casual observer of the problem. It's no place for the beginner or the faint of heart. If you're unsure of yourself, lack poise or confidence, you can expect to be eaten alive.

Slesinski says senior executives want to see the "big picture," a well-rounded overview that includes key aspects of a proposal or plan. They want to know the "bottom line" financial results of the project. They focus on such things as return on investments, asset management, marketshare, stockholder satisfaction, productivity/quality improvement, revenue increase, and attractive capital investment. In short, what's the payback?

They aren't interested in the intricate "mechanics" of the problem, nor how you achieved your results or how you arrived at the data, and they don't want to hear about the operational or technical considerations of the project. Save that type of information for middle management.

To better understand the difference between management levels, Slesinski makes these distinctions:

Senior Management	**Middle Management**
Focuses on:	Focuses on:
Asset management	Increased production
Return on investments	Personnel problems
Strategic planning	Better customer service
Research and development	Employee satisfaction
Increased marketshare	Overall cost control
Improved decision-making tools	Meeting monthly/quarterly forecasts
Stockholder satisfaction	Worker training
Long-term growth	Improving department status
Increased sales and profitability	Return on investment
New management techniques	Meeting schedules
Productivity and improvements	Reducing production waste and errors
Capital improvements	Information to operate properly
Reducing operation costs	Overall efficiency of departments

The mindset of senior management is strategic, financial, and long-term. The mindset of middle management is tactical, operational, and short-term.

Women who enter the executive arena must have thorough knowledge of the subject or problem, be well organized, and have answers to all of the above questions. She must appear confident and poised, have a positive attitude, and above all, she must never waste the time of a busy executive.

CHARACTERISTICS OF AN EXECUTIVE BRIEFING

An executive briefing has special characteristics. First, it's formal. That means you don't approach the executive briefing casually, but you don't have to be starched stiff either. Appear relaxed and comfortable while maintaining a professional manner. Focus on content with the purpose of persuading executives to buy into your proposal. Motivational or inspirational talks have no place here. This doesn't mean your speech has to be dry and boring. You can spice it up with interesting and exciting visual aids, by sticking to the point, and by following the rules of a powerful delivery such as eye contact, gestures, vocal variety, and physical vitality. Just demonstrating poise and confidence can be refreshing to executives, who must sit through many dull, boring meetings and speeches. And formal doesn't mean reading your speech. Nothing appears less convincing than a canned or read speech called the "talking head" syndrome. You may use notes, however. In fact, you can write out the entire speech if you have to, but refer to the notes only as a memory jogger.

Second, the executive briefing is concise and tightly organized. The information must be specific, to the point, and pertain only to the subject at hand. There is no room for extraneous information, long introductory openings, detailed analysis, or explanations of why you have come to make this presentation. Once you begin, get to the point and stay focused.

Finally, the executive briefing is short. If you can make your point in ten to fifteen minutes, good, but never take longer than thirty minutes. Yet be thorough enough to cover all aspects of the problem or proposal and include a question and answer session. Make each word count.

SURVEY RESULTS

Slesinski conducted a survey of eighty-six senior executives from large companies and found that fifty-five percent preferred to see overhead transparencies used as visual aids; 35 mm slides came in second. They liked the informality of overheads because they encourage discussions. The least preferred type of visual aid was motion film because it's not flexible, too impersonal, and too canned.

Most executive briefings are made in conference rooms to fewer than ten people; remember this when making your visuals. Make good-quality visual aids and use them sparingly.

With only thirty minutes to get your point across, you may have to supplement your talk with a handout. Most participants in the survey found handouts a distraction and often given out at the wrong time. Handouts can be distributed days before the meeting so those involved in the decision-making process can be armed with the up-to-date information needed to make decisions; or handouts can be passed out after your presentation to be studied later. Some believe it's not a good idea to hand them out immediately before your speech. One executive said, "People can get ahead of the presentation by flipping through their handout." It may be necessary, however, to distribute handouts before the presentation so participants can follow along.

Survey participants also said that handouts were too lengthy and detailed. Many didn't appreciate speakers who spent a lot of time going over information in the handouts as they spoke.

Fifty-six percent of the participants revealed they could forgive a speaker who displayed a slight nervousness during his or her speech, but they would rather see a presenter display poise and confidence, and have conviction in the products, services, or recommendations being presented.

Some of the major mistakes presenters made were listed as: presenting too much detailed and technical information, rambling on and on, using off-color humor or swearing, presenting a problem without a solution, and being arrogant and cocky.

Sure "turn-offs" were: being disorganized, having errors and inconsistencies in the information presented, being dull and boring, being unprepared, or not knowing the information. They didn't like presenters who were flippant or argumentative, made racial or gender slurs, directed their presentation only to a few, or who didn't listen to the feedback of the audience.

The "ultimate no-no," as Slesinski puts it, is for presenters to lie or give incorrect information instead of admitting they don't know the answer. Also, misrepresenting or slanting facts, being indiscreet by breaching a confidence, or lacking integrity were considered huge negatives.

What best influences executives? Here's what some said:

"Convince me of the tangible and intangible benefits of his/her proposal."

"Facts and data; understanding of my business; frank, honest answers to questions."

"Show me the sense of the proposal and show me the value of it for me and my company."

"Lay out all the alternatives and convince me that the recommended solution is the best one in the context of the overall business."

WHAT FEMALE EXECUTIVES SAY

Kathleen Vuchetich, Vice President and General Manager of West Ohio Gas, dislikes receiving a lengthy written proposal just before a presentation without a chance to review it. She suggests that detailed information be sent for review at least twenty-four hours before the meeting, freeing her to listen to the presentation. She says to include main points and detailed information in your handout if you don't have time to discuss them in your speech. This is often the case in executive briefings, when you may have two hours' worth of information and only twenty minutes to talk. A second time-waster, Vuchetich says, is to read word for word what is written on a visual aid.

Vuchetich suggests that speakers who offer to answer questions during a presentation should not shrug them off with, "I'll get into that later." It would be more appropriate to offer a brief comment on the subject and say that you will be going into detail on that topic later. Not answering the question can discourage other questions and irritate the questioner. She also suggests, if it doesn't throw you off, jump ahead to the portion of your presentation that will answer the question, cover the material in its entirety, then pick up where you left off.

Carolyn Elman, Executive Director of the American Business Women's Association, is annoyed by speakers who do not set up early enough, who don't know how much time they are allotted, and who don't start on time. She wants to know ahead of time what is to be discussed and what decisions are expected of her. She expects speakers to state their purpose and where they are going with the information they're presenting. Her advice: practice, practice, practice.

She also advises that beginners should consider copresenting. Work with another person who is experienced. It helps to lessen the nervousness when you share the stage.

Cathleen F. Oxner, CEO of Americom Bank, says the quickest way for a woman to ruin her credibility is to show a lack of integrity—not being truthful. She advises, "Never apologize for stumbling over your words or losing your train of thought."

Judith E. Gilbert, Public Relations Director for British Petroleum, says you can never insult your audience by taking less of their time. She advises speakers to do their homework. Know the audience and approach your topic from their point of view and adjust your style and information to their background. She stresses that no matter how many times she gives a speech, she always rehearses it again.

Joanne J. Bowsher, Executive Director of the Lima-Allen County Humane Society, offers this advice, "If you're nervous, speak as if there is only one person in the room."

Violet Meek, Ph.D., says "Give people cues so they know what they are going to listen to." Set them up with a clear organizational pattern they can easily follow. She suggests using an analogy so the audience can figure out what's coming. For example, with a baseball analogy you can use phrases such as, "we're in the final inning" to let the audience know you are drawing to the conclusion.

Meek says the logical progression is to tell a story from the beginning to the end, but that's backward. Because you have the greatest attention of your audience when you first begin to speak, begin with the most important point first. You should say, "Here, this is the finding. This is what I want you to know." Then fill in the details.

WHAT ABOUT HUMOR IN THE EXECUTIVE BRIEFING?

Humor in the executive briefing helps open lines of communication by breaking down barriers as it increases participation and motivation, softens criticism, and diffuses anger. Humor helps others see your point, illustrates an idea, and conveys a person's message in a nonthreatening way. Humor is the glue that bonds.

According to Joel Weldon, Toastmasters International 1989 Golden Gavel Recipient, "Humor should be part of your presentation no matter how serious the topic. Humor relieves tension and is suitable for any speech, as long as the material is appropriate." Although humor is appropriate in the executive briefing, it must be kept to a minimum. Use a brief humorous comment at the beginning of your presentation, then sprinkle sparingly throughout the presentation, but don't overdo it.

Some executives say humor has no place in the executive conference room. Nothing could be further from the truth. Don Seibert, former CEO and Chairman of the Board for the JCPenney Company, said, "The most senior people and virtually all of the chief executive officers with whom I'm personally acquainted have highly developed senses of humor. Humor is a common thread I've seen in thousands of meetings in different companies on the most serious of subjects. Humor helps you to keep your head clear when you're dealing in highly technical information or difficult decisions where choices aren't that clear."

And Robert Orben, former Director of the White House Speech Writing Department, 1976, said, "Business executives and political leaders have embraced humor because humor works. It enhances and projects a favorable image, eases tensions, influences thinking and attitudes, helps reassert control, and reduces the embarrassment of mistakes and awkward moments."

14

Meeting the Media

> *. . . one searches the magazines in vain for women*
> *past their first youth. The middle-aged face*
> *apparently sells neither perfume nor floor wax.*
> *The role of the mature woman in the media*
> *is almost entirely negative.*
>
> JANET HARRIS, *The Prime of Ms. America*

We have come to expect news broadcasts of world and sports events immediately. We want to know what is happening around the world and in our backyard, and we want to know *now*. Much of the information we receive comes by way of news conferences held to announce the opening of a new business or program, the promotion of a staff member, a presentation and recognition of an honor or award, an expansion of an old business, or a change in management. News conferences keep the public aware of breaking news involving national and local disasters.

If you are a member of a public relations department or if you represent your company in a formal capacity, you may someday find yourself facing the news media.

CONDUCTING A SUCCESSFUL NEWS CONFERENCE

You'll come off looking and sounding good if you know and understand what a news conference is all about. Again, preparation is everything. Here are suggestions for preparing and conducting a successful news conference:

1. *Ask questions.* What's your role and the purpose of the news conference? Are you to provide technical information, address a specific problem, announce a new product or service, inform of a change in management? Who will be there? Will you need visual aids to help explain the problem or situation? Is the room large enough to accommodate TV cameras? Is a microphone and lectern available? Will you have to meet with the media outdoors on location?

2. *When making an announcement, organize the information so the most important points are placed in blocks of time called "sound bites."* Keep the blocks of information together so the TV and radio reporters won't have to edit and splice pieces of the story together.

3. *Prepare and distribute a news release ahead of time that includes an agenda and fact sheet.* This allows everyone to get the same information at the same time and eliminates confusion. You will also eliminate receiving phone calls requesting additional information or clarifications.

4. *Approach the lectern with confidence.* Speak with authority. Don't stammer or hesitate. This is no time to let them see you sweat. Reporters have a sixth sense and know when you don't have the answers or are trying to evade sensitive issues.

5. *Because TV cameras might be present, don't use large gestures and don't stray from the lectern.* If you must refer to a visual aid, have it placed as close to the lectern as possible. Remember, only your words will be heard on radio. Your gestures and facial expressions won't add to your message. Choose the best words.

6. *Be brief and to the point.* Present an outline of the facts that says, "Here's what has happened, here's what I am going to tell

you." You should open with a strong statement of fact, and present your information in a well-organized and clearly focused manner. A news conference should not be longer than fifteen minutes and must have a structure and agenda. A spokesperson will often begin the conference with an opening statement that sets the tone of the conference, then turn the conference over to the expert(s), who will then give detailed information and answer questions, and finally, present a clear conclusion by summarizing the details.

7. *Each reporter will want an exclusive comment.* Be aware, if you consent to one reporter, you can become trapped and never get away.

8. *Answer questions in a positive manner.*

Do's and Don'ts of a News Conference

1. *Stay on track.* Don't allow the conference to digress or go astray. Don't buy into a reporter trying to throw you off. Have your facts straight and stick to your prepared script and don't waver from it.

2. *If several people are to present information, allow time for each to speak and give his or her area of expertise.* Limit the number of people to be interviewed to only two or three, however. The normal air time for a story is sixty to ninety seconds, so not everyone can be interviewed.

3. *Use visual aids whenever possible.* For good TV coverage, reports need clear, sharp visual aids to go along with the story.

4. *Make sure there is room on the lectern for several microphones.*

5. *Allow time for the reporters to ask questions, both during the conference and one-on-one afterward.*

6. *Be prepared for silly and negative questions, and be able to recognize an unfair question.* This is one situation when the audience may not be friendly. If a reporter asks a belligerent or unfair question, tell them the question isn't fair. Other members of the press will wait to see how you handle the question. If they see that it throws you off or intimidates you, they'll jump on you like a pack of wolves. The press will go for the jugular when they sense they can get a good story.

7. *When asked an off-the-wall question, it's best to say, "I understand your concern about this.* I don't have the answer right now, but I will get back to you." Then make sure you do. Don't give off-the-cuff unprepared answers. You will be in deep trouble every time.

8. *Know when to end the conference.* Reporters will continue to ask questions until they have bled you dry. When you have answered all relevant questions, restate your conclusion, then end the session. Reporters will most likely follow, wanting more. Don't refuse to talk, but politely refer to your previous remarks. They will respect that.

Tips for Defusing a Hostile Press

When faced with a critical situation, first, assemble the people who know what's going on and who have the facts. Gather all the information and make sure it's correct—not hearsay, rumors, or gossip. Your credibility is at stake. Make sure everyone involved is fully informed of the situation. Don't delay making a statement, or make it appear as though you are trying to stonewall. Get to the press before they get to you. Send a fax to the media with a statement about the situation, informing them that a news conference will follow. Then prepare the conference as soon as possible at a time that is convenient for everyone.

If you haven't had time to prepare to meet with the media, tell reporters you'll have information for them as soon as you get it. Offer a carrot of promise, then keep that promise. Tell them you haven't had time to review the problem or situation, but intend to do so. Nothing stirs the press more than the words *no comment.* If you don't have answers, they'll go to someone else less informed, and you may not like what you read or hear later.

Anticipate questions. An experienced reporter knows how to dig for information and ask pointed questions. Be ready to explain how the situation happened and what the company plans to do about it. Don't allow the reporter to put words in your mouth with questions such as, "Is it true you . . . ?" Don't answer any inappropriate questions. You have every right to decline a stupid question. If you are asked a question already asked by another reporter, answer by saying, "As I said before . . . ," or "As you may recall. . . ."

Reporters may shout their questions to you at the same time, making it impossible to hear or understand them. Set the guidelines at the beginning of the news conference. Let the press know how you want to handle questions. In most cases, they will comply. Sometimes a reporter will string several questions together. Reply by answering only the one question that allows you to make your point more clear.

Never make statements out of your area of authority. Let the experts answer those specific questions. Remain calm when faced with an antagonistic reporter. Approach him or her the same way you would any hostile audience.

Keep answers short. Don't give reporters anything they can latch on to and blow out of proportion. Never say something's "off the record." If you don't want to be quoted, don't say anything. Journalistic ethics have declined over the years since I got my degree in journalism. The once sacred "off the record" device doesn't work today.

Surviving the Impromptu

Being placed on the hot spot and answering questions that are hurled at you by members of the media can shatter the confidence of even the most experienced speaker. There will be those times, especially in news conferences, when you will be asked questions you aren't prepared to answer. But remember, you wouldn't be at the news conference if you didn't have specific information about an event or situation. Having all the information puts you in a much better position to answer questions, even though you may not have the information organized into a neat package. Impromptu speaking can be scary, but there are secrets to surviving the ordeal.

Here are a few tips for surviving questions hurled at you in a news conference:

• Listen carefully to the question. Restate the question to make sure you understand it.

- Take a second or two to formulate an answer. Take your time. Although it may seem like forever, pause and take a deep breath before answering; give yourself every advantage.
- Use the PRESS method for answering:

Position: Respond by stating where you stand on the issue or subject. State your position or viewpoint. What is to be accomplished? Are you for or against it?

Reason: Give the reason why you are for or against the issue.

Example: Give an example that illustrates your position.

Support: Support your position with statistics and facts.

Summarize: Give a brief summary of the main points of your position.

HANDLING THE TV INTERVIEW

That big television camera, with its staring red eye, can be intimidating. But it need not be.

If you are giving a report in a studio with no audience, look directly into the camera as you speak. Watch how news reporters seem to talk directly to you. Speak slowly and avoid large gestures; they'll be lost in close-up shots. Watch for the little red light on the camera to tell which one is focused on you.

If you are a participant in an interview, look at the person interviewing you. Talk to him or her as you would while sitting in your home discussing the day's events. If there is an audience, look at them once in a while and make eye contact. Avoid looking at the camera.

There will be many distractions with stage crews, monitors, and lights. Keep your attention on the interviewer.

Relax, but don't slouch. Keep your feet flat on the floor or cross your legs at the ankles, but never cross your legs at the knees. Keep your hands in your lap unless you are showing an object or feel a small gesture would be appropriate. Lean toward the interviewer and listen carefully to each question. Avoid all the distracting habits I have talked about before. Use good vocal variety, and *smile*.

Looking Good on Television

Appearing before a TV camera requires special attention different from that of your everyday appearance. TV anchor Holly Geaman says:

- Rub a small amount of Vaseline on your upper lip to prevent your lip sticking to your teeth.
- Avoid wearing white. Wear solid colors. Avoid prints with large patterns or polka-dots, plaids, and tiny horizontal patterns.
- Avoid flashy jewelry such as earrings, necklaces, and pins that could catch the lights and reflect into the camera lens.
- Tone down shiny spots on your nose and forehead with face powder.
- Wear slightly more makeup than normal, but don't overdo it. Lipstick is a must. Avoid blue eye shadow. Keep colors in the warm tones of tans and browns.
- Eyeglasses will glare in studio lights. Tilt your head down slightly to reduce the amount of glare. Remember photosensitive lenses will darken under hot studio lights. You may want to change them to a regular pair.
- Always assume that the microphone is on and say nothing you don't want to go out over the air.

Understanding what the press wants and needs to cover the story, knowing how to handle the questions, hostile or otherwise, and knowing what is expected of you, will help you relate information more effectively, confidently, and professionally.

15

Making an Introduction

*Challenges make you discover things about yourself
that you never really knew. They're what make the
instrument stretch—what make you go beyond the norm.*

CICELY TYSON, The Quotable Woman

"**A**nd now, here's Johnny!!"

Who hasn't heard those words? For years Ed McMahon's introduction of Johnny Carson on the *Tonight Show* became a signal to get ready for a comedian to appear and make us laugh. And he did.

"And now, here's Betty!!"

It doesn't work. What's the difference? Johnny Carson became a household word and needed no introduction. But nobody knows Betty. Who is she? What does she do? What's her experience? What does she want from us? Why should we want to listen to her? A good introduction will answer those questions.

Now, the shoe is on the other foot; it's your turn to introduce the speaker. Where do you begin? Are you going to "wing it"? No. You're going to prepare as you would for any speech. Ask the speaker if he or she will provide you with a written introduction. If they tell you to just say anything you want—don't.

THE IMPORTANCE OF INTRODUCTIONS

So, what's a good introduction? It's a mini-speech, less than a minute, but contains all the elements of a speech—opening, body, and conclusion. The introduction acts like window dressing, enticing the listener into the store. The introduction builds a bridge between the audience and the speaker as it sets the mood and tone for the speech to follow. It provides vital information about the speech and speaker to help the audience get ready for what's to come.

Introducing a speaker is much the same as introducing two people at a party. You give them leads so they won't stare blankly at each other with nothing to say. You tell each of a mutual interest, forming a bond between two strangers. The same is true when you introduce a speaker. You draw the audience and the speaker together so they can communicate. Your introduction serves to:

• give information about the speaker's special qualifications, expertise, knowledge and experience on the subject. This is where you can build his or her credibility.

• make a transition from other speakers and events helping the audience to emotionally shift gears between the last speaker or event to the next.

• set the mood for the audience. Favorably predispose the audience toward the subject. The introduction should tell the audience what to expect. Is the topic serious or humorous? Let the audience know they can settle back for an hour of fun or that they must put on their thinking caps and help solve or analyze a problem. Tell the audience how the information will be of value to them by answering the question, "What's in it for me?"

• arouse the audience's interest. Give them a reason to want to listen to the next speaker.

- clarify the speaker's purpose. Will the speaker inform, inspire, motivate, entertain? Have you ever found yourself listening to a speaker and wondering why the speaker was talking?
- make the speaker feel welcome.

The Introduction Format

The Opening. Just like the opening of any speech, the opening of an introduction must grab the audience's attention and make them want to listen to what you have to say.

"Our speaker today is, ah, Bill Johnson, and ah, he is going to talk about, ah, well, something important, and ah, well, here he is." Would you want to be introduced in that manner? If you say, "Our next speaker is going to knock your socks off," you better have a good reason for making such a bold statement. If the speaker's topic is darning socks or handling explosives this opening might work well. If the weather is cold and the speaker is known for her humor, you may bring that into your opening remarks with something like, "The weather may be cold outside, but our speaker will generate enough hot air to make the room cozy."

"Our speaker today walked across the continent of Africa" gets my attention.

The Body. This is where you give specific information about the speaker and the subject. Tell the audience why they should listen and why the speaker is talking to them now.

A good introduction should explain the following four why's:

1. *Why this subject:* Will the information presented help make the audience rich, famous, more beautiful?

2. *Why this speaker:* This is the time to build the speaker's credibility. Let the audience know why she's the best person to talk to this audience. Is she an authority? Has she discovered a miracle cure? What education does the speaker have? Does she hold a degree in this topic? Basically, the audience wants to know who this person is and why they should listen to her.

Find something of a personal nature about the speaker that will generate interest. Did the speaker solo an airplane at age fifteen or win a chili cook-off? This information may not directly relate to her topic, but gives the audience more insight into the qualities and capabilities of the speaker. Be creative and innovative with the introduction.

3. *Why this audience:* Tell why this audience should be interested in this topic. Do they have a personal stake in it? Why should they listen? Why do they need this information?

4. *Why at this time:* Does the audience need this information now? Why? Will next week be too late? Tax preparation information isn't as urgent in the fall as it is before April 15.

All four of these ingredients should be included in your introduction, but not necessarily in this order.

The Conclusion. And now, a drum roll, please. This is the easiest part of the introduction and leads directly to the presentation of the speaker. One sentence will do. As you give the cue for the speaker to take control of the lectern, raise your volume and say, "And now, please help me welcome (the drum roll) . . . Cathy Jones" (the cymbal crash) or "I proudly present . . ." or "Give a warm Texas welcome to. . . ." And if you want to follow up on the remark about the cold weather you might say, "And now to start warming things up, I am pleased to introduce. . . ."

Anything that feels comfortable to you and that lets the audience know now is the time to applaud will work. But always, I repeat, always let the last thing you say be the speaker's name.

NINE NEVERS

1. *Never tell how much you know about the speaker's subject by making your own speech on her topic.* A minister was asked to address the graduating class in a small town. He wondered why he had been chosen. On graduation night, the principal began his introduction, "Reverend Smith doesn't know it, but about a year ago I was in his community on a Sunday and heard his sermon. His sermon was so fine, I knew that this

was the man we wanted to speak to us at our next graduation exercise." And for the next five minutes he gave a full account of the speech he had heard the previous year. Little did he know that the address in the minister's pocket was the same one.

2. *Never ramble on and on.* Be brief—an introduction should be no more than one minute, although some speakers may require a bit more. Dorothy Sarnoff, author of *Speech Can Change Your Life*, says, "It would be a rare person indeed whose introduction required more than three minutes." Extremely well known politicians and actors need little in the way of introduction. In most cases, the more famous the person, the shorter the introduction. What more needs to be said than, "Ladies and gentlemen, the President of the United States."

3. *Never try to be cute by taking jabs at the speaker, her profession, background, or how she's dressed*—unless the purpose of the gathering is a roast or you are introducing a very close friend where everyone knows everyone else. If you do use this form of humor in an introduction, make sure that everyone understands the jab is made in fun and not meant to embarrass the speaker. A friend of mine is known for always wearing a hat. You can spot her in any crowd. She has a sense of humor, and has taken many jabs about her hats. Mentioning her hat in the introduction would fit well.

4. *Never tell personal stories about yourself and the speaker.* Don't tell about the time the two of you got lost at the shopping mall. Telling personal stories leaves the audience feeling left out of the inner circle and somewhat offended.

5. *Never overdo the praise.* The Talmud advises, "Only a fraction of a man's virtues should be enumerated in his presence." Overpraising gives a false impression and higher expectations than the speaker may be able to deliver.

6. *Never mispronounce the speaker's name or title.* A memory haunts me about the first time I introduced a speaker, and I still cringe from the experience. I didn't mispronounce the speaker's name, I just called him by the wrong name. I intro-

duced Joseph Black as Joseph Stonewell. I have no idea where that name came from. My only defense is I was young and inexperienced. Today I have no such excuse. If you can't pronounce the speaker's name, ask her to pronounce it, then write it out, spelling it phonically. Krakowiak becomes Cra-*co*-v-ack. Underline or mark the accented syllable. Dorothea Johnson, protocol and etiquette consultant says, "If you are going to introduce someone, call ahead to verify the speaker's exact name and title."

7. *Never tell falsehoods about the speaker just to build his or her credibility.* Don't give wrong information. Make sure you have the speaker's correct occupation, hometown, and the title of the speech.

8. *Never refer to the speaker as the wife of So-and-so.* Mary should stand on her own merits, not those of her husband.

9. *Never try to "wing it."* The chances are you'll fail. Amy Childes relates an introduction she once got when speaking to a group of insurance adjustors that went something like this: "Our next speaker is Amy Childes. I don't remember the title of her speech, but she's here to talk about something."

Dale Carnegie said, "Most introductions are poor affairs, feeble and inexcusably inadequate." Never attempt to make an introduction without first preparing and practicing it. And finally, practice and practice, then practice some more. Where have you heard that before?

INTRODUCTION COURTESIES

1. *Greet the speaker upon her arrival and make her feel welcome.* Find something you can compliment her on, such as how nice she looks. I don't care how far we have climbed that corporate ladder, we are still women. We like to hear we look nice, especially when another woman says it. Telling her how good she looks on the outside will help build her confidence on the inside. Tell her how much you look forward to hearing what she has to say. It's always a boost to be told the audience wants to hear you. Don't let her sit or stand off by herself unless she tells

you that she needs a few minutes to collect her thoughts. Place yourself in the speaker's shoes.

2. *Remain at the lectern until the speaker arrives, then lead the applause.*

3. *Make her feel welcome by smiling and shaking her hand.*

4. *Readjust the microphone for the speaker if she's much taller or shorter than you.* Don't let her fumble with the microphone. Help her make a good first impression.

5. *Always walk around behind the speaker to take your seat.*

6. *Take your seat away from and out of sight of the speaker.* Never stand off to one side in view of the audience; it's distracting.

16

Serving as Emcee

Women are challenging and overturning the status quo
and recasting social, economical, and political trends
of today. Momentum is moving in our favor.

PATRICIA ABURDENE, *Megatrends for Women*

Your role as master of ceremonies is to take charge of the proceedings at a special event. You are like a conductor of an orchestra who knows exactly what note every instrument is to play and when. You set the mood and pace, introduce speakers, and put guests at ease. You're in charge of leading the program by announcing when events will occur. You must coordinate the meal, band, press and photographer, et cetera. You are responsible for seeing that everything happens when it is supposed to. In other words, you are the glue that holds the event together. It's a big job, requiring hours of preparation, detailed planning and organization to insure that everything goes off without a hitch, but if you can keep your boss and employees on schedule, get the kids on the school bus on time, or plan a three-day conference, you can easily be the emcee.

A good emcee is well organized, good with details, entertaining and witty, has a good voice, and presents herself with confidence. She must be skilled at making introductions, able to take command, and have common sense and good taste.

TWENTY-THREE QUESTIONS TO ASK
BEFORE YOU BEGIN

The answers to many of the following questions may seem obvious or redundant, but it never hurts to repeat the important points.

1. *Who is the coordinator of the event?* Someone planned this event. It could be the president of the club, the program director of the company, or a meeting planner. He or she knows the reason for the gathering, has decided what is going to happen, who will do what and when, and has created the agenda. He or she will have a list of special guests, know who is to be at the head table, the name of the entertainment and honorees. Make this person your right arm. You will coordinate everything with the coordinator. Your job is to take what the coordinator has put together and make it work. Another person you want to stay in close contact with is the sales director or banquet coordinator of the facility where the event is held. They know how to get the things you need.

2. *What is the event?* Award or retirement ceremony, a roast, a national conference banquet, an annual get-together or celebration? Each one will have its own atmosphere, standard format, and customs to be followed. An anniversary may be dignified, a roast outrageous, and an awards ceremony formal. Your job is to set the mood and tone.

3. *When is the event?* An awards luncheon can be quite different from a dinner ceremony. Normally, a luncheon will be shorter, with a lighter meal and fewer activities. A dinner ceremony may be followed by a band and dancing.

4. *Where is the event?* A large convention center, hotel ballroom, or small banquet hall? Each presents special challenges. Most facilities are well equipped to handle large crowds quickly.

5. *Who will be seated at the head table?* The head table can be as large as twenty people or as few as six. Those seated at the head table have a special honor or function. Generally, the

emcee, guest of honor, speaker, chairperson, president, directors, clergy, and spouses or escorts are seated at the head table with the chair of the event sitting closest to the lectern. The other guests are seated in ranking order. The rule is, the more important or higher the position, the closer to the lectern. The emcee sits to the right of the lectern as you face the head table and the keynote speaker to the left. Guests are seated on the side of their spouses or escorts away from the lectern and should always be included in the introductions.

6. *Who will be speaking?* If the speaker(s) hasn't given you her introduction, get it. You learned how to do that in chapter fifteen. Get each name correct. Spell it out phonetically if you need to and practice pronouncing any difficult names. Know her title and position within the company.

7. *How much time will each speaker need?* If the speaker is the keynoter, plan on her speaking about forty to fifty minutes, but ask to make sure. Most likely a keynoter is experienced and knows how to time her speech; however, if the speaker is a long-winded award recipient you could be in trouble. Ask before the event begins how much time he plans to speak. If he shrugs his shoulders, that's a cue for you to tell him he has a specific amount of time.

8. *Will the speaker need visual-aids equipment?* Where does he want it placed? Work this out well ahead of time. Don't wait until the middle of the program to start moving table and chairs to set up a viewing screen.

9. *Are there special guests in the audience who should be recognized?* Not everyone can sit at the head table; there just isn't enough room. Yet many people deserve recognition for their help making a program possible. They could be past officers of dignitaries. Again, get their names and titles correct.

10. *What are the seating arrangements?* Most events will involve a meal, so you can plan on round tables with as many as ten people per table or long tables butted together to accommodate hundreds. Why is this important? If the event is an award ceremony, you must allow time for people to maneuver around tables to get to the front of the room to receive their award.

11. *Will there be a microphone?* The answer had better be yes. Never conduct a program without one. Most often the microphone is attached to a table lectern placed in the center of the head table. Sometimes a floor microphone is placed beside the lectern. Both are troublesome. They don't allow you room to move or to turn your head to speak to each side of the room. Ask the banquet coordinator to provide a microphone that can be detached from the holder. You'd be surprised how many microphones are fixed on a gooseneck stand.

12. *Who is the guest of honor?* Once again, get the name and title of the guest of honor and pronounce it correctly. Make sure he is welcomed and shown where to sit.

13. *What protocol will be followed?* Some organizations follow a specific format at their ceremonies. Learn the procedure for this group. Do they always introduce dignitaries? Do they have a special toast or tradition? Do they say the Pledge of Allegiance or sing the National Anthem? If a toast is to be made, by whom and when? Do your homework.

14. *What type of dinner will be served?* Buffet or sit down? Each requires a different amount of time depending on the amount of people to be served. Allow at least an hour for dinner either way when making your agenda.

15. *Will a invocation be given and by whom?* Is the person a clergy or lay person? Sometimes the clergy is seated at the head table, sometimes at a table near the front of the podium. Find out.

16. *Will there be an open bar?* When will it be open? Normally, the presence of a bar is obvious, but when it is to close isn't. Announce that the bar will be open for only five or ten more minutes, allowing guests time to get their drinks. This also signals that the program is about to begin. Announce when the bar will reopen, usually at the end of the program.

17. *Will there be breaks?* If the program is long, yes. Plan on a break after the meal. Announce that guest have fifteen minutes before the program begins.

18. *Will awards be given?* Awards and recognition may be the highlight of the day. You'll need to know how many awards are to be given and if someone else is to take charge of this portion

of the program and announce the recipients and hand out awards or certificates. Make sure you have the name of the award correct. Find out if the recipient(s) is expected to come to the microphone and make a speech. Is the guest of honor the only recipient? Is this a surprise award or honor? If it is, the recipient most likely won't be prepared to make a speech, so don't put her on the spot. Plan extra time if photographs are to be taken.

19. *Are there smoking regulations?* More and more buildings and events are smokeless these days, but still there are folks who haven't gotten the message. You may have to announce at the beginning of the program that smoking is not allowed.

20. *Does anyone need special assistance getting to and from the podium because of a a disability?* Someone who has difficulty walking won't be able to manage the steps. Ask the banquet coordinator to place a ramp at one end of the podium. A wheelchair-bound speaker or awards recipient won't be visible behind a lectern. Ask that a microphone be set up and placed off to one side to solve this problem. Another reason for a handheld microphone. Also, see that a table is positioned to accommodate a wheelchair.

21. *What should I wear?* Business dress or formal gown? Find out what the custom is for this event and group. Often the event will dictate what you wear. Obviously, if you are the emcee for a formal dinner celebration and the men at the head table are dressed in tuxedos and the women in long gowns, you aren't going to wear a business dress.

22. *Will there be special entertainment?* The band or entertainment tops off the event. Once introduced, your job is over. But there are exceptions. I've seen vocal groups entertain as part of the ceremony. They need an introduction and you need to know how long they will perform. If a band is to play, when will they set up? You certainly don't want them coming in during the program, setting up their equipment, and testing microphones. As professionals they know how much lead time they need to accomplish this. Check with them. A band may be present to play as guests arrive or to play during the meal. You need to know when they are to begin and end.

23. *What are the names of the personnel staff responsible for the banquet room?* They have been with you all evening attending to your every need. Thank them. Arrange with the banquet coordinator to have all the wait staff step out of the kitchen for a round of applause for their service. Mention them all by name if practical.

With all this information, arrange the program so that events flow smoothly and that everything happens on schedule. It could take days, even weeks, to organize and coordinate the program thoroughly. So begin planning well in advance.

TIPS FOR CONDUCTING A SMOOTH PROGRAM

Arrive early. Make sure that everything is in place and ready to go before guests arrive. Check with the staff to see if dinner will be on time, and that there are no surprises. See that all guests, speakers, dignitaries, and guest of honor are present.

Your opening remarks should be light, friendly, and humorous, creating a festive mood. You can use any of the twenty-two grand openings mentioned in chapter 3, and give them a twist that will fit the occasion. In some cases, you will be the first person to step to the lectern, and you will not be introduced. Begin by letting the audience know who you are. "Good evening. I'm Mary Smith" (give your title or position whichever is more appropriate).

This is a good time to tell a story. It can be about almost anything, but a story that directly relates to the occasion and the audience works well, and of course it should be humorous. Introduce the head table from your right to left and from lowest ranking to the highest.

Give an overview of what will happen and when. Explain any special or unusual proceedings for the guests who may be unaccustomed to them.

The main thing is to get the festivities off to a warm, comfortable, and funny start.

A printed program will help everyone, especially you, follow the order of the agenda.

If you see that time is running short and you are presenting a long list of names for recognition, ask the audience to hold their applause until all parties have been recognized. Sometimes you will still get applause. You must stand tough and repeat the "No Applause" request. After all, it's your responsibility to stay in control and have the event end on time.

Always thank those responsible for the program, all the guests, the speakers, food servers, and hotel staff. Announce that the main event is over and everyone can now enjoy the entertainment.

Prepare, prepare, prepare.

17

Persuasive Speeches

> *It is impossible to persuade a man who
> does not disagree, but smiles.*
>
> Muriel Spark, *The Prime of Miss Jean Brodie*

Women have always been the great persuaders—behind the scenes—and not since the suffragettes have women been more outspoken. Women's voices raised in unity during the 1970s led the way to women being heard as individuals today.

Many methods exists for getting someone to change or maintain a behavior, perception, belief, or emotional state. Holding a gun to a person's head is one method, and this may be effective for a time, but it's not very wise in the long run. When trying to persuade, you need a more lawful method.

Whether trying to persuade your boss to give you a raise; convince city council to build better roads; or persuade someone to buy or boycott a product or service, vote, volunteer, or support your candidate, you'll be more successful if you understand a few basic principles of persuasion.

Every persuasive appeal has four basic elements: a claim or proposition; evidence to support that claim; a sound reason for how and why that evidence supports your claim; and finally, a move to action.

Along with these elements are what the Greeks called "canons of proof." The three canons are: ethos, referring to moral character; pathos, meaning emotion; and logos, meaning logic. When the four elements of persuasion are combined with the three "canons," you have a persuasive method that is not only lawful but powerful.

TEN STEPS TO PERSUASION

Professor Alan H. Monroe, developer of the *motivated sequence,* suggests five steps for persuasion. I have taken his work and expanded on it.

1. *Get the audience's attention by stating what needs to be done.* As with any speech, you need to get the attention of the audience with a strong opening. Not all of the twenty-two grand openings suggested in chapter 3 will work here. Since your purpose is to persuade a reluctant audience to consider a serious matter, I suggest you use a straightforward approach—no gimmicks. Address the topic in a manner that gives the audience necessary information about the subject and at the same time brings their attention to the subject.

Make a concise statement about the problem to establish your purpose and help the audience understand the magnitude of the problem. For example: "This city, with a population of only 45,000, has a crime rate four times as high as the largest city in this nation. The occurrence of over 190 burglaries, 3 homicides, 49 reported rapes, and 750 assaults in this city last year reflects a problem that needs to be addressed." So far this is just a statement and must be backed with evidence to support it. This statement sets the tone of your speech as it tells the audience why they need to know this information.

2. *Define the problem.* Describe the problem and discuss its seriousness: "Our present city budget does not allow for an increase in police manpower. As a result, many of our streets go unpatrolled at night, causing an increase in burglaries. We need more and better police protection."

Defining the problem is best achieved through a logical approach. Although you need to excite the audience throughout the speech by appealing to their emotions, keep in mind that an exclusively emotional appeal could easily turn people off. Furthermore, emotions can't be sustained for the desired length of time needed to achieve results.

Remember how you felt after watching a sad, tearful movie on television? The sadness lasted about as long as it took you to get to the kitchen to make a snack before the next program came on. The same will be true for the folks in your audience. You may get them fired up with emotion, but it will probably fade on the way to the parking lot, and will likely be forgotten by the time they get home. So you need to present your proposition with logical reasons supported by facts the audience can take home and act upon later.

3. *Explain the origin of the problem.* What is the history of the problem or situation? How did it begin? Who started it? "The increase of teenage gang activity throughout our city is one cause. . . ."

4. *Show that the problem exists by giving solid evidence that supports your proposal.* There are three types of evidence: direct, verbal, and real. Using direct evidence you could cite newspaper articles and police reports. Verbal evidence can be testimony from rape or assault victims. Real evidence is photographs or video footage of a crime scene with a sheet-covered body lying on the sidewalk.

Facts need to be supported by solid evidence. Quote experts such as the police chief, and official documents such as police reports. It is always best to give several sources from which you have taken your information. The evidence you give must be conclusive. Be careful not to make generalizations. Presenting factual, verifiable evidence not only supports your claim, but increases your credibility.

5. *Explain the magnitude of the problem.* Statistics quoted must be verifiable, and should not be used alone without a basis for comparison. For example, "More than one hundred robberies occurred last year." Is this a lot? Is it below average for a city this size? Show the statistics for other cities of the same size. Without a comparison, your audience is left to wonder the sig-

nificance of the statistics, or they could think they're being mislead by slanted information.

6. *Present your solution.* You have presented the problem; now you need to offer a solution. State what needs to be changed, such as an attitude or belief; or what needs to be done, such as writing letters, making phone calls, or voting. "In our case for safer streets, my solution is to have more police on the streets at night between the hours of midnight and 6 A.M." Make clear what you think needs to be done to solve the problem, and be specific. Include information that tells why and how your solution will work and how your solution will benefit the city.

If you have had personal experience with the success of this solution, explain how it worked elsewhere. Illustrate how your proposal meets the needs for solving the problem. For example, "An increase of seven percent in the income tax of our neighboring city has allowed for additional police and better equipment, resulting in the reduction of that city's crime rate last year by fifty-eight percent."

7. *Give proof your solution is best.* Cite how your solution has worked in other cities and what the results were. Give statistics, affidavits, and testimony of those who also know your solution will solve the problem.

8. *Help the audience visualize how the problem will be resolved using your solution.* Show what life would be like with your solution or what it would be like without it by drawing a graphic and colorful mental picture in their minds. For example, "If the budget for the police department is not increased, we will find ourselves faced with a higher crime rate and less protection for our property as the community grows. The city will decay into a slum controlled by street gangs. People will not be safe to leave their homes at night."

9. *Explain why other solutions will not work.* Anticipate objections and be prepared for opposing views. You might suggest some objections yourself to show you see both sides of the issue and can be fair.

10. *Show how your solution can be accomplished.* Lead the audience to take action by summarizing, using a quote or illus-

tration, by providing additional inducement, or issuing an emotional appeal. If your speech has been designed to make people aware of a social value that needs changing, you will need to change their beliefs about the subject. In some cases, your goal will simply be to reinforce the way they think about the topic.

If your speech calls for action, ask your audience to do something specific, such as write letters, make phone calls, or sign a petition. Lastly, allow the audience to follow your lead by telling what you plan to do about the problem. "We must get behind our police department. I ask each of you to vote, as I am going to do, for the increase in the city income tax to insure safer streets for our community."

These steps will give you a start in understanding how to deliver a persuasive speech. With a little practice, you can become skilled in the art of persuasion.

THE SPOILS OF PERSUASION

There are many ways to sabotage a perfectly good speech. I have mentioned many ways throughout this book, but one more important area remains. Audiences can be led to believe almost anything if you present the information in a convincing manner, but let a fallacy slip into your speech and you stand to ruin an otherwise wonderful presentation. A fallacy is, according to *The Reader's Digest Great Encyclopedic Dictionary*, "an erroneous or misleading notion; an unsound or incorrect belief or judgment; a deceptive quality; or any reasoning, argument, et cetera, contrary to the rules of logic." Don't fall prey to these fallacies and ruin your credibility and lose your argument.

1. *Gross generalizations*—Statements suggesting that what you say is a universal truth. Words such as *all, everything, everyone* signal generalizations. For example: "Everyone I know uses Brand X detergent."

2. *False reasoning*—Whether inductive or deductive, false reasoning occurs when making a statement based on illogical assumptions. For example, inductive: All the houses on our street have a garage; therefore, I conclude all houses everywhere have garages. An example of deductive reasoning: All

houses are made of brick. This is a brick; therefore, it will be used to build a house.

3. *Jumping on the bandwagon*—Just because the majority may believe something doesn't make it true. Statements such as, "Everyone believes . . ." or "All your neighbors are racing to buy . . ." should send up a red flag.

4. *Ambiguous words and phrases*—Words such as *sometimes, maybe, perhaps,* don't give the precise information needed.

5. *Name calling*—You accomplish nothing by attacking another person's character to prove your point.

6. *Misleading statistics*—Some say you can make a statistic say anything you want it to. Using statistics based on improperly gathered information, too small a sampling, misinterpretation of the results, and limited data can skew information.

7. *Weak authority*—Suggesting something is correct based on the word of another person who may not be an authority on that particular subject weakens your argument.

8. *False consequence*—This occurs when you draw a conclusion based on imaginary results. For example, "If we don't rid our streets of crime, gangs will move in next door."

A perfectly good speech can be ruined by trying to manipulate and slant evidence that misleads the audience. As a woman speaker, you don't need to add doubts and questions about your integrity or character by using faulty examples and statements.

18

Special Occasions

*We cannot have expression till there is something
to be expressed.*

MARGARET FULLER, *A Short Essay on Critics*

THE AFTER-DINNER SPEECH

Anytime a speech follows a meal, it's called the "after-dinner speech," whether it follows breakfast, lunch, or dinner. It's presented in a social atmosphere that is pleasant, relaxed, and friendly. After-dinner speeches are made at class reunions or the celebration of anniversaries; it can also be part of a business conference or meeting. The audience expects to be entertained while being informed, inspired, or motivated. The delivery should be upbeat, jocular, lively, and enthusiastic. An after-dinner speech is lighthearted, with about eighty percent of it humorous. It should reflect the fellowship of the group, but it can also have a serious underlying message. Speaking after a meal presents a challenge as the audience sits digesting food, dozing off.

As you prepare your talk, remember:

1. *Keep your speech short.* Twenty minutes is about as long as anyone can sit and listen to a speech after a meal without becoming uncomfortable. Any longer could be hazardous to the kidneys.

2. *Speak in a conversational tone, friendly and warm.* Keep your speech positive, with plenty of examples and anecdotes to illustrate your message.

3. *Build a theme into the speech.* A theme could be the fear of flying with a humorous twist, safety in the workplace, or a motivational message on aspiring to greatness through perseverance. This is no time to get on a soap box and plead for a personal cause. Stay away from a heavy-handed, emotionally charged message. All the audience wants after dinner is to be entertained for a few moments.

4. *Use humor.* Even though your message is built around a serious theme, it can be demonstrated in a humorous way. Be sure that your anecdotes and jokes relate directly to your theme. Remember, we learn best while having fun.

5. *Keep your language simple, clear, and easy to understand.* The audience isn't going to follow a complicated message while basking in the creamed chicken and melon parfait.

THE KEYNOTE ADDRESS

A keynote address reflects the reason for the conference or gathering. It sets the tone of the meeting, and usually has several key points with stories that illustrate the message. A keynote presented to a group of writers would include stories of hard work, dedication, rejections, and success. In an address to doctors, the message could be about the advances being made every day and the difficulty keeping up with technology.

Keynote addresses are motivational or inspirational. They review the past, define the present, and look toward the future. The best type of opening is to refer to the audience and occasion, remarking on a common interest. The delivery is strong yet enthusiastic. The conclusion should inspire and uplift, and leave the audience feeling good.

Consider it an honor to be asked to present the keynote address. It means you are held in great esteem and respected for your ideas and ability to speak.

The keynote address is normally forty-five minutes in length.

PRESENTING AN AWARD

Awards are given for almost everything, from Woman of the Year to the student selling the most book-cover protectors for the high school band. This is a pleasant task and you can do it with ease by following these steps:

1. *Give a brief history of the award.* If the award is an established one, explain how the award was founded. Tell when the award was established, by whom, and under what circumstances. If this is the first time the award is being presented, explain why the award is being given at this time.

2. *Tell what the honoree did to deserve the award.* Did she sell the most nuts, work the hardest, volunteer the most hours, or go beyond the call of duty? Relate personal insights into the character of the honoree that show why the person is deserving of the award.

3. *Present the award.* There isn't any mystery here. Call the person forward and say something such as, "Mary, on behalf of all the members of the Volunteer Auxiliary, I take great pleasure in awarding you this plaque for your twenty-five years of devoted service." Then hand her the gift or award. Help her open the gift if it's wrapped, and then dispose of the wrapping paper. Shake the recipient's hand and give her room to step to the lectern for her response. You need to be sensitive to the person's nervousness. I always ask, under my breath, if she wants to say something. Most people will, but occasionally I sense sheer terror in the eyes of the honoree as she realizes she's expected to say something. Don't push or embarrass her. An easy out is to announce that, "Mary is so choked up right now she just wants to say thank you to everyone and she'll talk to you individually after the program."

Make your speech before calling the person front and center. Don't have her stand there while you sing her praises, making her feel uncomfortable.

If awarding a plaque or certificate, hold it so that everyone can see it. Read the inscription or message, and never reveal its value.

ACCEPTING AN AWARD

Probably some of the best (or worst) examples of accepting awards are at the Academy Awards every spring. The long-winded acceptance speeches have become the butt of many jokes and a headache for the producers of the event.

Take a cue from them and keep your speech short. There is no need to gush on and on about how grateful you are. Just say thank you and express your gratitude for the honor. Here's where I always blush. (I hate it when that happens.) When you are with a group of other women, looking humbled and blushing will be overlooked. But please try not to look coy, shy, and undeserving when presented an award by a man or in the presence of men. I don't want to sound off, but, ladies, we must overcome that little-girl notion. Learn to accept praise. The "I'm not worthy" is a false notion. Accept the award with a sense of honor and pride while keeping your tone sincere.

Give recognition to those making the award possible. Refer to the gift, plaque, certificate, or trophy. Say that you will display it proudly in your office or in a place of honor in your home. If the award is a wrapped gift, open it and show it to the audience.

If you feel that you worked exceptionally hard for the award, or if you were in competition for it, mention how your competitors also worked diligently for the honor—that just by having the competition, everyone benefited. If you were singled out for exceptional service, mention your indebtedness to all those who worked closely with you.

Tell what the honor means to you, how you have benefited from the experience of working with everyone, the friendships you have formed, and then close with a brief look toward the future as the club, company, or organization grows.

If the award has been kept secret, you may not be prepared for this honor. Here's where your skills at impromptu speaking will come in handy. Keep this section in mind and prepare now. I have faith that someday you will need this information.

THE WELCOMING SPEECH

There are many situations that call for a welcome speech. As a city official you may be asked to welcome newly elected members to the council, or welcome new members to your club or company. You may even welcome the bride or groom into your family. To make someone feel welcome, use the following steps:

1. *Announce the name of the person being welcomed.* That shouldn't be difficult, but make sure you have the correct pronunciation. Express on behalf of the group that you are pleased they have decided to join your club or your company.

2. *Give background information.* This will take some work. The best way is to call the person and get the necessary information. Find out about his or her achievements. Include information about family and church affiliation. Does she belong to other service or professional organizations? Does he have special interests and hobbies? Include all this information, if appropriate.

3. *Extend the welcome.* Close with a remark about how the members of your club or organization look forward to having the new person join and how much he or she can contribute to the goals of the group.

Just as you would when presenting an award, don't put the newcomer on the spot by asking him or her to speak.

THE FAREWELL OR VALEDICTORY SPEECH

Most often we think of a valedictory address as given at a high school or college graduation ceremony, but it can also be the parting message given to any group, business, or organization from which a person retires or leaves. The basic formula follows the structure of other speeches with an opening, body, and conclusion.

The opening can be humorous or serious, but as always, it should be sincere. The body should include four elements:

1. *Tell about your experiences with the organization.* Talk about what it has meant to work for the company and with the people. Mention people by name and explain how and what they did for you. Tell how you grew from knowing them. Recall the good times, and even mention the hard times, with fond memories.

2. *Talk about what you gained by working with this company or volunteering for this organization*—education, life experience, friends? Mention the friends who were influential in your success.

3. *Let them know where you hope to go from here.* Tell what your plans are for the immediate and distant future. If retiring, tell how you plan to set the alarm clock to go off as it has for the past twenty years, then stick out your tongue at it, smile, roll over, and go back to sleep.

4. *Express gratitude and goodwill toward the group you're leaving.* Offer your sincere wishes that the company or organization continues to prosper and grow. Wish everyone good luck and good health. Thank everyone for their friendships and cooperation. Express how you feel about leaving and how you will miss everyone.

The conclusion can be one of looking toward an optimistic future for yourself and those you leave behind, an uplifting inspirational message, or a goodwill prediction for everyone. Keep the conclusion light and brief without getting teary. This might be difficult, especially when your feelings run deep.

THE NOMINATING SPEECH

Time after time, I have heard someone stand and say, "I want to nominate Mary for president," then sit down. Ladies, this is not a nomination. A nomination should describe the duties of the office, why the person you're nominating is deserving of the position, and her qualifications for the job. Nominations can be brief when everyone knows the qualifications of the individual or no other person is running for office; or it can be very formal using all the techniques of persuasion, but whether you are nominating someone for a national political office or a local service club, follow these five basic steps when making a nomination:

1. *Begin by naming your candidate.* This is a simple statement. For example: "Madam president, I would like to nominate Mary Jones for the office of president." Nothing difficult about that.

2. *State the job description.* Obtain the job specifications from a presiding officer. Most clubs and organizations have a standing list of duties for each office. Aside from the job specifications, announce special skills needed to perform the duties, such as good communication and listening skills, honesty, and being well organized. You might want to include her genuine concern for the growth of the organization.

3. *Explain how your candidate meets all the qualifications, training, and experience for the job.* This is an important step. Show by example how she understands the responsibilities and duties of holding that office and how she can meet the demands of the job. Give a brief summary of other jobs your candidate has held within the organization. Tell how the organization gained twenty new members as a direct result of her efforts as membership chair. Tell about her personal involvement with the organization, her long-term commitment to the community, and how she has devoted many hours to the continuing growth of the club. For example, "Mary has been a member for seven years. When she first joined she didn't hesitate to jump right in and volunteer for the newly vacated position of bulletin editor, where she did an excellent job."

You could even comment on other activities outside of your organization in which your candidate has worked or volunteered. What about her activities in fund-raising for her church? Mention her family and hobbies, even her love of animals—if you think that will get a vote.

4. *Use the persuasive punch.* Here's where you illustrate how the club or organization will benefit with Mary at the helm. Explain how, with Mary's experience in public relations, the club will benefit because of her ability to work and deal with difficult people. She knows how to smooth ruffled feathers. Show how she has been a benefit to other organizations, how she brought

about change, or how things improved because of her influence. Make your claim without exaggerating her qualifications.

5. *Make the formal nomination.* Again, you want to repeat your candidate's name by saying something like, "It gives me great pleasure to nominate for the office of secretary-treasurer, Mary Jones."

The nominating speech should be given with enthusiasm, dignity, and conviction.

DEDICATIONS

A dedication, according to *The Reader's Digest Great Encyclopedic Dictionary,* is "to set apart for a sacred use or devote to any special duty or definite purpose; to inscribe or address as a compliment; or to open or unveil to the public with a formal ceremony." With that in mind, approach the dedication in a dignified and formal manner without being solemn. It's a proud moment and should have a positive tone.

There are two types of dedications: those dedicating an existing building or structure to the memory of someone, usually a well-respected citizen, and those dedicating a new building or structure. In a dedication of a building to a person, you want to concentrate your talk on that person, his or her contributions to the community and how this building will forever stand in memorial to that person.

For an impressive dedication follow these steps:

1. *State the purpose of the dedication.* Open with a brief explanation of the purpose for the gathering. For example, "Today we are gathered to honor the memory of one of our most outstanding citizens and pay tribute to the contributions she made to our community."

2. *Honor the person.* Announce the name of the person being honored.

3. *Tell about his or her accomplishments.* This is the body of your speech. Enumerate the person's generosity, such as donating money to the community, especially to the education system; or how he or she struggled to build a successful business that helped the city grow. But better still, weave his or her accom-

plishments into stories that best illustrate how this person's accomplishments made the community better.

4. *The dedication.* This is the conclusion of your speech. Formally dedicate the tablet or marker that will be attached to the building. For example, "Therefore, we dedicate this building to our community so that it may further serve as a place of education to all." Conclude with eloquence and inspiration. A quote works well here.

With the opening of a new building, focus your talk toward the future of the structure. There are four parts for dedicating a new building:

1. *State the purpose of the dedication.* Give a brief introduction relating to why everyone has gathered. They'll know this, but say it anyway.

2. *Describe the building being dedicated.* A new wing of a hospital, a reception area to an art gallery, a playground, gazebo in the park, or even a flag pole. Tell about its function, how it came to be, its size and beauty.

3. *Relate the value of this building.* Talk about its merits and how, as a symbol of caring, the building will serve the citizens. Tell how the community will benefit from the structure.

4. *The dedication.* Close with an inspirational message of hope for the future. For example, "Today, we dedicate this playground to the service of our children so they may grow in strength and develop a sense of fair play." Again, a quote always works well.

THE TRIBUTE

The purpose of the tribute is to show appreciation for someone with admirable qualities, values, and moral character, or who has reached a milestone in life. A tribute (sometimes called a eulogy or testimonial) is an expression of praise that chronicles someone's life and singles out his or her qualities. It provides comfort. Most often, eulogies are given as a memorial to the dead, but not always. A tribute can be made at any time to anyone deemed worthy. It can be made at a twenty-fifth or fiftieth wedding anniversary, after a successful election campaign, in celebration of a seventy-fifth or one-hundredth birthday, at a mother-daughter dinner, or in honor of a long-time volunteer who has given many years of public service to the community. A tribute can even be given to a loved one returning from military service.

It should include the individual's achievements; essential facts of the person's life; his or her background; and contributions to family, friends, and community. Like the dedication, it is formal, delivered with dignity and respect.

Here is a simple plan for giving a tribute or eulogy:

1. *State the purpose.* The audience most likely will already know why they are there, so a long introduction isn't necessary. Simply confirm the reason for the gathering. For example; "We are gathered here today to pay tribute to one who has passed on, but who has left many footprints for others to follow."

2. *Tell about the deeds and accomplishments.* This is the body of your speech where you recall the deeds of the individual such as large contributions to the community in the form of volunteering time and money to charities and projects; but the deeds can also be small in nature, such as being a Big Brother or Sister, playing in the community orchestra, or helping the elderly. Mention the person's interests, hobbies, organizations, and church affiliations.

There is always some good to be found in everyone. Mention positive character traits. You may have to dig deep in some cases, but make the effort to discover what the person has done.

3. *Talk about the person's good character, special contributions to family, friends, community.* Was she a veteran? Did she serve with honors? Tell stories that demonstrate these qualities. Surely, you won't want to mention his or her grouchy nature. Look for the positive. Was he or she pleasant to be around? Did that person always have something positive to say? Did he encourage others beyond adversity? Was she educated? Could he show tact and humor? You can mention his strengths and weaknesses; after all he was human. Maybe the weakness was a fault, such as spending so much time in the service of others that she neglected her health. But don't try to justify the person's death.

As I stated earlier, humor is always appropriate, even in a eulogy. Perhaps your friend was an avid fisherman. A remark made in good taste about Joe liking to fish and a story that recalls a special fishing trip will relieve the tension.

4. *Reveal a little-known piece of information or nice secret.* Keep it positive.

5. *Close with dignity and on a positive note.* Keep it brief and inspirational. You may quote something that the deceased was known to say or include the philosophy he or she lived by.

This may be the only acceptable time for not making direct eye contact. Seeing someone cry brings me to tears. Never accept the offer to give a eulogy if you feel that emotion will overtake you during the speech. This is extremely difficult when eulogizing a child. You will have to rely on your innermost feelings as a woman for this difficult task. The audience needs to look to someone strong to give them courage in a time of sadness. If you begin to feel your throat tighten and tears swell in your eyes, pause and take a deep breath. Let the emotion pass or have someone standing by to take over just in case you can't continue.

Keep the eulogy brief at five to eight minutes. And, as with all speeches, practice.

A TOAST

A toast is a mini-tribute to a person or group. It is most often rendered in a lighthearted manner, with humor fitting the occasion. It can be in the form of a rhyme, limerick, or doggerel. The situation and the occasion will determine which you choose. A birthday party for someone turning forty can be silly with toasts that match. A wedding and anniversary dinner has a particular gay mood. In the past, toasts were offered with an alcoholic drink and it was considered an insult, or at least in bad taste, to toast with water, but today with fewer and fewer people drinking, it has become acceptable to toast with fruit juice, milk, even iced tea. If you don't drink and nothing else but wine or alcohol is available, toast with your water and fake it.

When making a toast:

1. *Refer to the reason for the gathering.* For example, at a wedding, "Today, we celebrate a wonderful occasion—the marriage of Joe and Mary."

2. *Refer to the honoree(s).* A toast can be presented to anyone or anything. While attending formal dinners in the military, toasts were made to all ranking officers, the president of the United States, and the country. If toasting a bride and groom, you could say something about how they met, for example.

3. *Express goodwill toward the honoree(s).* Let them know they are welcomed to the community as husband and wife. Wish them happiness for the future.

Many books are filled with short, snappy, and deeply moving toasts. Finding an appropriate toast shouldn't be difficult.

The most common toasts are made at weddings where the bride, mother of the bride, and the bridesmaids are toasted. Although anyone can make a toast, most commonly the bride is toasted by her father, a close friend, or best man.

Here are a few different toasts for a wedding:

Here's a toast to the lovely bride,
And to the husband by her side.
Here's to the home they're going to share;
May love and trust dwell with them there.

or

Let us drink to the health of the bride,
Let us drink to the health of the groom,
Let us drink to the Parson who tied them
And to every guest in this room.

or

Here's to the health of the happy pair,
May good luck meet them everywhere,
And may each day of wedded bliss
Be always just as sweet as this.

or

To the bride and groom—
May their troubles be only little ones.

or

To the bride and groom—
May your coming anniversaries be outnumbered
Only by your coming joys and pleasures!

or

To sister on her wedding day:
We've toasted the mother and daughter;
We've toasted the sweetheart and wife;
But somehow we missed her,
Our dear little sister—
The joy of another man's life.

Conclusion

I hope you'll never have to face an audience with trepidation. This book has provided insights into how you can begin to control the nervousness that accompanies you to the lectern. As you become more experienced, you'll gain confidence and truly begin to believe in yourself. You'll never have to say, "I'm afraid I'll make a mistake and look foolish," "I'll bore the audience," "I fear my mind will go blank," "I'll look stupid," "The audience will see I'm not a very good speaker," or "My voice gets shaky and people will see I'm nervous." Those days will be long forgotten.

Never turn down an opportunity to say a few words. Each speaking experience helps you grow. Accept that challenge with a willingness to face fear head on, and never allow it to conquer you. Commit to excellence in whatever you do. Never say it's good enough. Try harder. Discipline yourself to do the best you can and never allow self-doubt to creep in.

See you on the platform.

Index